BUSH TUCKER MAN

STORIES OF EXPLORATION
AND SURVIVAL

BUSH TUCKER MAN

STORIES OF EXPLORATION
AND SURVIVAL

LES HIDDINS

an
ABC
BOOK

For their assistance in the writing of this book grateful thanks to:
Dr Andrew Cook, London; Dr Karen Cook, London; Alison Coote;
Frank Dalton; Dr Femme Gaastra; Peter Gesner, Queensland
Museum; Steve Harris; Caroline Hiddins; Dr Peter Isdale, Australian
Institute of Marine Science; James Cook University Library Staff; Karl
Roth Museum of Central Australia; Jack King; Bob Lasseter; Dr Glen
McLaren, Richard Walker and Howard Whelan.

Special thanks to Rosy Whelan for her invaluable assistance in the
preparation of the manuscript itself.

Published by ABC Books for the
AUSTRALIAN BROADCASTING CORPORATION
GPO Box 9994 Sydney NSW 2001

ISBN 0 7333 0546 6

Designed by Kaye Binns-McDonald
Set in 10½/20 pt Goudy Regular by
Midland Typesetters, Maryborough, Victoria
Colour separations by First Media, Adelaide
Printed in Hong Kong by Quality Printing

5 4 3 2 1

CONTENTS

INTRODUCTION

So what's the connection between Bush Tucker and Australian History? Quite a lot when you start to think about it, and that point comes out pretty quickly once you look at the yarns contained here. So many of Australia's explorers set off trying to do this or that, and died as a result of ignorance. They were quite unaware of the survival resources that this new country they were trying to explore had to offer them. Burke, Wills and Kennedy are prime examples of what I'm on about here, and a lot of the problem was not just ignorance but also cultural arrogance to a certain extent. Many of these individuals carried a swag full of prejudices with them on their journey and finally were forced to pay the price for it. On the other hand, those who decided to roll with the countryside and to take the land for what it was were often quite successful, and here my mind goes immediately to the likes of John McDouall Stuart and his band of men.

But the one thing we must always remember is just how young this country of Australia really is. I'm not talking about the geography of the landscape, but rather about the modern form of the country. European presence here is only brand new, and

we are still learning about our backyard, so to speak. To give it some perspective, white settlement has been established here barely two hundred years now, and I myself have been present for nearly a quarter of that time. In many ways we are only scratching the surface, and we should be very careful that we don't in fact carry our own form of cultural baggage with us as some of those early explorers did. We think we know the country, but we are only kidding ourselves—of course we know very little in reality. Our arrogance and our ignorance lead us to believe that we do understand it, but that's not really the case . . . not by a long shot.

On that note, I sometimes have to wonder if the age of discovery and exploration is really over. Somehow I doubt it, and in particular here in Australia. Here, you can still manage, if you try hard enough, to plant your feet on the ground in some remote and isolated corner of the continent, and be pretty sure that you are the first white person to actually stand on that particular patch of dirt. Now just try doing that exercise in England or Europe. While we can still do something like that, we have a long way to go and an awful lot to learn.

Learn your country
Les Hiddins
Townsville 1996

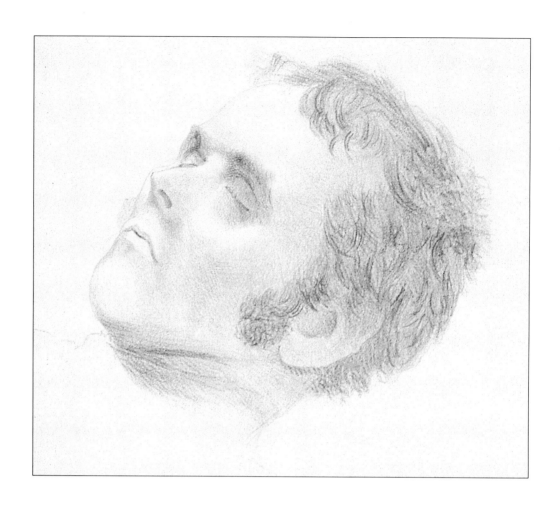

Irishman Alexander Pearce was transported to Australia in 1819 for stealing six pairs of shoes. After escaping with seven other prisoners from the savage Sarah Island convict settlement, he survived an arduous journey across Tasmania through a nightmare of cannibalism. Pearce was sentenced to death and went to the gallows in 1824. In his own defence he claimed that No person can tell what he will do when driven by hunger.

CHAPTER ONE

THE CONVICT CANNIBAL

I LOVE HISTORY, because it tells us about our past, and that helps us understand things going on around us today. The story I'm about to tell you would have to be one of the goriest pieces of Australia's history. It's set in Tasmania's lonely wild country—a long, long way from my favourite haunts up north. So, let's go on a trip back in time—back a couple of hundred years in fact—when the British arrived in Tasmania, or Van Diemen's Land as it was known then.

The remote island was a magnificent, isolated, untamed wilderness, inhabited by a couple of thousand Aboriginal people, and the British saw it as a perfect place to dump their worst convicts.

Looking around today it's hard to imagine the brutality of those times. But the Brits were hell-bent on creating savage prisons, and 'civilising' the place. Part of that 'civilising', of course, meant dealing with the local Aboriginal population—rounding them up or shooting them.

Most people have heard of Port Arthur on Tasmania's east coast, and it's a great place to go if you want to get a feel for colonial convict life. But if you think Port Arthur was tough, there was another place right across on the wild west coast, about four hours' drive from Hobart, which they reckon was the most feared convict prison in Australia.

Looking at it from

The British built a penal
settlement, designed to be the
worst possible prison for convicts
who reoffended, on remote
Sarah Island in the early 1820s.
To help create a bleak inhuman
world, the island was stripped of
all vegetation. Prisoners were
punished by unremitting labour;
floggings and bashings were par
for the course. It was a hellish,
brutal place, created to break the
toughest men.

a military point of view—and it was the military who were in charge of the convicts—Macquarie Harbour is the perfect prison. The environment itself forms the prison walls: endless rugged mountains on one side and the Southern Ocean on the other. As a surveyor who went there in the early days of settlement said, *so completely shut in is this harbour by the surrounding, closely wooded, and altogether impractical country, that escape by land is next to impossible.*

The authorities figured there'd be no escape from Sarah Island at the top end of the harbour, so a convict settlement was founded there in 1821. The only way to get to Sarah Island was by boat, through the Harbour entrance, or Hell's Gates as the convicts called it. Rightly so, too.

You see, the idea was to punish prisoners by simply unremitting labour. Floggings and bashings were par for the course. It was a hellish, brutal place, designed to break the toughest men.

Apparently, back in those days, there used to be thousands of swans floating around the harbour. The soldiers used to hunt them in their spare time, just for fun or out of boredom. They used to eat them too, along with stuffed wombat and fried echidna. The message was pretty clear around that part of the world, whether you were an Aborigine, a convict, a swan, a wombat or an echidna. So much for the first site of European settlement on Tasmania's west coast.

But back to our prisoners. Six days a week, at sunrise, work parties of convicts would leave their cells on Sarah Island to row to the top end of the Harbour and up the Gordon River. Their job was to cut down the precious stands of Huon pine growing in the rainforest that still runs down to the river's banks to this day.

They didn't cut down all the trees—they were just after the tall, straight ones. You see, they needed wood to make ships, and Huon pine (or *Lagarostrobos franklinii* as the boffins call it) is a pretty special tree. It grows only in Tasmania, and it particularly likes the south-west region. Besides being Australia's longest-lived species of tree—some have been aged at 2300 years—it's very resistant to rotting in water because of its oil content; the oil puts shipworms off too. So what you've got is a slow-growing softwood that's quite light, easy to work with and very stable. It's not prone to expanding and shrinking the way some timbers are. You can understand why they wanted it for shipbuilding.

Mind you, the prisoners probably saw it in a different light. The men were forced to work through the winter, cutting down trees, rolling them to the water and rafting them to Sarah Island. They worked from dawn to dark, with very little food and totally inadequate clothing. On returning to the island at night, the worst prisoners were made to wade ashore through the freezing water and sleep in their wet clothes. Scurvy, dysentery and rheumatism were rife, and it's no surprise that many of the men tried to escape.

One of them was a bloke called Alexander Pearce, an Irishman who was transported to Australia in 1819 for stealing six pairs of shoes. He arrived at Port Jackson with a ship-load of convicts in early 1820, but was sent on to Van Diemen's Land, where there was a shortage of labour at the time.

We don't know much personal detail about Pearce, but we do know what he looked like, as one of the convict artists drew a sketch of him after he'd died. Not such a bad looking bloke according to the sketch. He wasn't very tall (but none of them was in those days) and he appears to have been in his late twenties when he arrived in Hobart Town.

Once there, Pearce worked at a few different jobs, but he just couldn't stay out of trouble. He didn't commit any really serious crimes, but he had a habit of pinching things, and he ran off and hid in the bush a couple of times. He was also found 'drunk

When Alexander Pearce and his mates escaped from Macquarie Harbour, they had absolutely no concept of the journey that lay ahead. This view shows the type of landscape that confronted them: a series of mountain ranges choked with scrub, intersected by steep valleys and rushing rivers. These days it's the heart of Tasmania's World Heritage Area wilderness country.

I haven't spent much time in the mountain ranges of Tasmania's south-west but what I find really interesting is that at the time of Pearce's escape Aboriginal people were still moving through this country, surviving on bush tucker.

Pearce's journey from
Macquarie Harbour to Shannon
Hut, a phenomenal undertaking,
took him across rugged mountain
ranges in the vicinity of
Frenchmans Cap, a distinctive
landmark that lies to the east of
the Franklin River.

and disorderly' about town now and again when he was supposed to be in the watch-house. By July 1822, the authorities had had enough and he was sentenced to spend the remainder of his term—about four years—at Macquarie Harbour.

In late September, about a month after arriving there, Pearce was in a work party at Kelly Basin, a little bay in the Harbour just a short boat ride from Sarah Island. He and half a dozen others were cutting down Huon pine, and they made a decision: they were going to escape. The first thing they did was to pinch a couple of boats. Pretty crude boats they were too. They didn't have much in the way of supplies—virtually nothing in fact—but the one thing they did have was an axe.

The seven escapees made their way west along the northern shore of the harbour to the convict coalworks. There they stole some provisions—a bit of flour and beef—and were joined by another escapee, Robert Greenhill. They planned to sail out of the harbour in one of the boats and around the coast to Hobart Town. But not long after setting off, they thought they were being followed, and they panicked and put ashore.

The first thing they did was to chop up the boat and get rid of the sails. With escape by sea no longer an option, they were forced to travel overland. Even today, all that area to the east of Macquarie Harbour is wilderness country. There are no sealed roads and no houses—just wild mountains, fast-flowing rivers and tangled forests. It's challenging country, and moving through it is a real adventure. You need to be self-sufficient and know what you're up against.

The escaped convicts, of course, had no bush skills and precious little food. They had no maps either—they were literally feeling their way. But I guess when you think about it, probably just about anything would have seemed better than staying on Sarah Island.

Well, normally that would have been the case, but not this time. The convicts had absolutely no concept of how far their journey might be. Remember that when they escaped, the country between Macquarie Harbour and the eastern settled districts was completely unknown to the white settlers. The escapees started their journey by climbing over 1100 metres to the top of Mt Sorrell, where they spent the night, lighting a fire for warmth and taking turns to keep watch. To them, the distant mountains looked easy enough to climb. But before long, reality struck home.

To their horror the eight men quickly discovered what lay ahead. The ground was rough and covered with thick scrub, the weather was wet and foggy, and the nights incredibly cold. In order to make a better escape, they decided to keep to the high ground. But in that area it's hard to stay up on the high ground, because travelling east means continually crossing mountain ranges, going up, then down, then across rivers and through valleys choked with scrub. Even the rainforest country can be intimidating, with tangled, fallen trees covered in mosses and ferns that create an impenetrable, three-dimensional maze.

With so little to eat, their clothing torn and feet reduced to pulp, morale quickly faded. It wasn't long before desperate, gnawing hunger set in.

Now, I haven't spent much time in those parts, but what I find really interesting is that at the time of Pearce's escape, Aboriginal people were still moving through that country, surviving on bush tucker. According to the experts, there's plenty about, but you've got to know what to look for and how to find it. Some things are hidden, like the fungi that grow underground and in fallen logs, and the small, starchy underground tubers of ground orchids. These tubers are about the size of your fingernail, and you can dig them up and eat them raw. There's a whole range of small berries, including native currants, climbing blueberries and mountain berries. They might look poisonous and some of them have an astringent taste, but I'm told they're quite nutritious.

Stinging nettles grow in the limestone country along the rivers. Boiling them neutralises the stinging hairs, and they make a nutritious vegetable feed. Bracken is edible too, so long as you roast or boil it first. Unfurling palm fronds are also good tucker, and they reckon the pineapple grass that grows on the heights is really tasty, as is the nectar of the banksia flowers amongst the eucalypt scrub.

Besides the plant life, there are plenty of animals too. The rivers and rainforests of south-west Tasmania attract wallabies, ringtail possums, Tasmanian devils, and a whole range of other species. Eels and platypus live in the water and there are mobs of birds around too—kingfishers, swans, boobook owls, cockatoos and sea eagles. Up on the higher ground are wombats, and of course snakes are not exactly uncommon.

When the British first set eyes on Macquarie Harbour on Tasmania's west coast, they saw it as the perfect prison: endless rugged mountains on one side and the Southern Ocean on the other.

But gathering bush tucker and hunting or trapping animals is full-time work and it needs the knowledge, skill and support of a tribal social network. The convicts had none of this. With their scant supplies dwindling, what were they to do? On the eighth day, in sheer desperation, three of the men turned back. You can imagine how desperate they must have felt if they actually chose to return to Sarah Island. As things turned out, it was a smart decision.

The rest of the men continued on, but just as they crossed one mountain range, another would appear. Even today there's no easy way through that country. The mountain ranges trend in a north-west—south-east direction, but many of the river systems cut across the valleys, forming natural obstacles. The rivers are fast-flowing and dark, stained with tannin from the button grass vegetation. And these rivers can rise suddenly—up to five metres in four hours—without warning.

In wet weather it's a pretty gloomy place. Low mist hangs over the peaks. Water drips off the scrub, and as you push through it you get absolutely soaked. It can be really oppressive, especially over a few days. The men would have had patches of good going through the open rainforest adjoining the rivers. But the so called 'horizontal scrub' would have slowed them right down. It looks a bit like bush country that's been blown over by a cyclone, except that that's not the case of course. It grows that way quite naturally I'm told, but it's a devil of a thing to try to walk through, and around that part of the world, there's plenty of it.

These days tourists flock to the south-west corner of Tasmania to admire the landscape. Some of the hardier ones get out and hike through the mountains or raft the wild rivers. Funny, isn't it, the way one man's meat is another man's poison? Mind you, travelling through parts of the south-west area is a bit easier now, mainly because of the four-wheel drive tracks built back in the '70s and early '80s when the Tasmanian Government was surveying for a dam. You see, these rivers are a hydro-electrical engineer's dream. The plan was to build the dam below the junction of the Franklin and lower Gordon Rivers, about halfway between Strathgordon and Macquarie Harbour, right in the heart of Wild Rivers National Park.

The proposed dam caused quite a bit of a stir in its day because it would have flooded most of the Franklin–lower Gordon river system, and (combined with a dam across the King River) would then have submerged the vast, spectacular wilderness to the west of Frenchmans Cap. Powerlines, roads and quarries would have followed. Instead, the protesters moved in, the media followed and the Franklin dam blockade, as it was known, became the biggest conservation battle in Australian history.

When the dam was being planned, some of the conservationists decided to really check the place out. One of them was a keen caver and he made an incredible discovery along the banks of the Franklin River—a chamber that was about 20 metres long, by 12 metres wide and 5 metres high, now known as Kutikina Cave. All over the orange clay floor were ancient stone tools and charred bits of animal bones. He'd accidentally discovered an Aboriginal occupation site that had been totally untouched since who knows when.

Until then, there had been a debate amongst the academics as to whether or not Aboriginal people had actually lived in Tasmania's remote south-west in the past. But following the discovery of Kutikina Cave, a series of expeditions to the middle reaches of the Franklin River uncovered more than 20 caves, along with several thousand stone tools and all sorts of bones, mainly from wallabies and wombats. Carbon dating of the charcoal and other bits and pieces proved conclusively that Tasmanian Aborigines inhabited these caves for more than 5000 years.

In fact, further study has revealed that use of the caves probably started 20 000 years ago, ending abruptly 14 000 years ago, when the world's glaciers began to melt at the end of the last ice age.

It's fascinating stuff when you think about it. You see, back when the caves were in use, that whole area looked very different from the way it does today. Macquarie Harbour was dry and the coastline lay some distance to the west of its present location. Obviously the climate was a lot colder—in fact they reckon the valleys of the upper Franklin basin were filled with glaciers, and that icebergs floated off the Tasmanian coast!

For the conservationists, the discovery of the caves clinched the deal. Kutikina was quickly established as the southernmost known habitation of people anywhere on earth during the last ice age. In 1983, the Federal Government stepped in and the dam idea was dropped. By now south-west Tasmania was well and truly on the map.

More recently, other clues have been found that suggest when the white men first arrived at Macquarie Harbour, Aboriginal people travelled from the west coast right through to the east of what is now the Wild Rivers National Park. They didn't live permanently in the south-west, but they used it as a transit zone to move between the coast, where seafood was plentiful, to the midlands, which were full of game. Well-trodden footpaths allowed them easy access through the scrub, and as we've seen, there was plenty of tucker along the way.

But the convicts didn't know about the footpaths or the bush tucker, and after fifteen days of unimaginable hardship, hunger, exposure and sickness, somewhere around the Loddon Plains area, the hell of Sarah Island gave way to a new nightmare. With nothing left but the axe, the men were driven to a desperate extreme. Alexander Pearce's later confession makes chilling reading:

> We were famished for the want of food, and began to intimate to each other that it would be much better for one to be sacrificed for food for the rest, than the whole of us to perish. We cast lots as to who should suffer.

Well, they'd made the decision. They'd decided to start eating each other: cannibalism. According to Pearce, it was Greenhill who was the instigator of the whole thing. He was the one pushing and promoting the idea. Greenhill had apparently been in this situation before, and on that occasion he'd been the executioner. 'Tastes like pork,' he reckoned, and he volunteered for the job again.

It might be interesting to have a look at the power structure of this mob. Now Greenhill had a mate with him, a bloke called Traviss, who was his partner in crime. Apparently they'd been convicted together for stealing a schooner in the Derwent River. Seeing that Greenhill carried the only axe and Traviss was his mate, the other men gave them a bit of respect.

While Greenhill set about killing Bodenham, the bloke who'd drawn the short straw, he sent the others off to collect wood and build a fire. I don't think we need to go into all the gory details, but after they'd cut up and cooked the body, the remaining men survived on the meat for the next four days. They were still crossing mountainous country and had no other food.

After they'd recovered from the initial shock and disgust at what they'd done, it

It's not often that Tasmania's south-west coastal regions look as tranquil as this, just south of Macquarie Harbour. Lashed by roaring forties gales and high rainfall, this area is still only sparsely populated.

was inevitable that there'd be more killings. But things took an interesting turn. One of the men, Mathers, got sick. (No wonder, after what he'd eaten.) Greenhill took this as a good opportunity to sneak up on him from behind and whack him over the head with the axe too. But Mathers must have had a thick skull, because the blow didn't kill him—it just stunned him for a bit. Once he got up again, he insisted that Greenhill be forbidden to carry the axe, as he was obviously not to be trusted. What an amazing situation this must have been. Someone comes up and hits you over the head with an axe when you're having a bit of a nap, and all you have to say about it is that he can't be trusted to carry the axe.

Mathers, despite his sore head, was smart enough to realise that as Greenhill and Traviss were mates, the only hope he had was to team up with Pearce, and this is what happened. But it didn't last long. Pearce had also worked out that there'd probably be another killing, and it would be either he or Mathers who'd get the chop, so Pearce got friendly with Greenhill and Traviss. You can imagine how Mathers would have felt about that!

Now Mathers had no choice but to keep his distance from the others and to keep an eye out for his life. But a couple of days later while he was resting, the others jumped on him and killed him with the axe. Once again they cooked and ate the body.

The three remaining men still had no idea how far they were from the settled districts, so I suppose Pearce must have been starting to feel a bit nervous. The going was easier now, although there were still more mountains to cross. It was at this point things took a very interesting turn. About four days after they'd killed Mathers, a snake bit Traviss's foot and his whole leg swelled up. It was pretty tough trying to climb mountains in that condition, and eventually Traviss was unable to continue.

Needless to say, Traviss was a bit concerned about his future, and quickly pointed out to Greenhill and Pearce that they still had enough of Mathers left to get them back to civilisation. And in case this wasn't convincing enough, he decided the time was right to remind Greenhill that they were mates.

We've been companions for so long a time both in days of Prosperity as well as in the present days of Adversity where we always communicated to each other our Intentions and

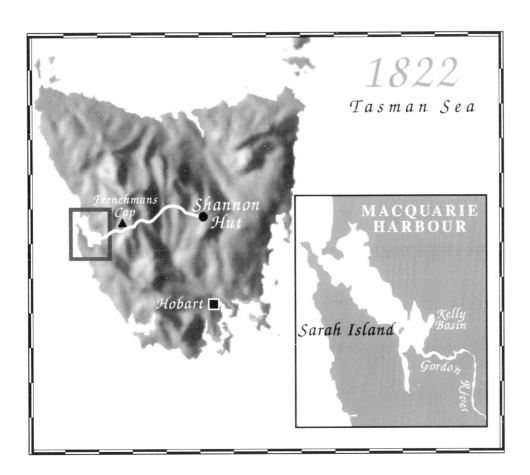

determinations of every subject and have intrusted each other with the most guarded secrets—I trust and hope that you will not delay time in waiting for me but proceed on your Journey and leave me where I am that I might have an opportunity of making my peace with my Maker.

Greenhill took pity on Traviss and spent the next five days with him in the hope that he'd recover from the snakebite. This was not a very relaxing time for Traviss, mind you, who watched every move Pearce and Greenhill made. Perhaps Traviss should have reminded his 'mates' that as he'd been bitten by a snake, the poison by now would be all through his body—a bit of negative psychology.

By the sixth day, Greenhill wanted to get going, so he promised Traviss he'd help him on the way. Well, it was a pretty slow day's travel, with the inevitable mountains, valleys and rivers to cross. By the time they made camp for the night, they were all exhausted, and the unfortunate Traviss fell into a deep sleep. By this time, Greenhill and Pearce had worked out that they weren't going to make it much further if they had to continue to carry Traviss.

Poor old Traviss woke up in the middle of this discussion and knew straight away what was going on. He did his best to persuade them not to kill him, but before long he fell asleep again. I'll leave you to work out what happened next.

With only two men left and one axe, Greenhill and Pearce swore they were the greatest of friends. They were convinced they must be getting close to the end of their journey and when, a few days later, they came to a huge open plain, they were sure it was a stock run. They were bitterly disappointed to find this wasn't the case.

However they made another discovery once they'd crossed the plains: they saw smoke. As they drew closer they heard human voices, but were unable to make any sense of the conversation. According to Pearce's later confession, they'd come across a group of Aboriginal people. Pearce reckoned that there were about 40 or 50 in the group and they were armed with spears. He claimed that he and Greenhill ambushed the Aborigines and, brandishing the axe and a big stick, frightened them away.

At the time, the Aborigines had been feasting on kangaroo. Pearce and Greenhill took as much of this tucker as they could carry and cleared out. It must have made a welcome change from human flesh.

They'd now been on the run for over a month, and there was still no sign of civilisation. Never in their wildest dreams did they imagine their journey would take so long. On they went, wondering if they'd somehow taken a wrong turn.

They were soon out of tucker again, and as Greenhill was keeping a firm hold of the axe, Pearce started to get a bit nervous. Wonder why. Night was the worst time, so to protect himself, Pearce would set up his own camp a fair way from Greenhill's. One day, however, the two men spotted smoke again and, figuring it was from another Aboriginal fire, planned their attack. They waited till nightfall and then surprised the camp of 20 or so who were enjoying a feast of kangaroo, birds and possums.

There's been some discussion over the years as to whether or not Pearce and Greenhill really did carry out these ambushes, but it's certainly possible. The way I see it is that the two men had the element of surprise on their side. And they would most probably have been the first white men the Aborigines had ever seen.

Fearing that French interest in the Pacific might lead to settlement on Australia's far north coast the British established a military garrison, called Victoria settlement, at Port Essington.

*Leichhardt and his men would
most probably have skirted
around the edge of Red Lily
lagoon country—a magnificent
stretch of Arnhem Land wetland
country.*

inset *This rock art gallery near Oenpelli, Arnhem Land, shows some of the outside influences that inspired the local Aboriginal artists. The fishing boat is an image of a Macassan prau, used by the beche-de-mer fishermen who came to northern Australia to collect sea cucumbers for trade.*

On their way to the British garrison at Port Essington, the Leichhardt expedition passed through Arnhem Land's Oenpelli region, an area rich in natural beauty and outstanding Aboriginal rock art.

Cobourg Peninsula—the final leg of Leichhardt's journey to Port Essington. The entire Cobourg Peninsula is now encompassed by Gurig National Park.

Magnificent mud crabs from the Cobourg Peninsula area are a real treat.

With food in their bellies and more in reserve, the men's attitude quickly changed. They became friends again and that night were able to share a camp site. A few days later, a big mountain came into view. The men were convinced it was Table Mountain, at the edge of the eastern settled districts they were headed for. They knew that Table Mountain lay pretty well due east of Macquarie Harbour, and this made the job of navigating a whole lot easier.

Now in the early 1820s, Hobart Town was a rough and ready kind of place. The population was between 2000 and 3000, including prisoners, military and free settlers. There were a couple of hundred houses at most, and they were pretty basic—either simple, two-roomed cottages or wattle and daub huts. There were no proper roads and the small township was still surrounded by scrub.

Generally only the very worst prisoners were sent to Van Diemen's Land. They were under the supervision of the 48th Regiment of Foot. All sorts of encouragements were given to convicts who showed signs of towing the line, and those who did were allowed to get out and find jobs of their own. But the system often backfired, and plenty of prisoners escaped into the bush, as Pearce himself had done on more than one occasion.

Bushrangers were a real menace, especially for a government that was trying to encourage settlers to move out of town. Later on, the bushrangers were hero worshipped and became an important part of Australian folklore, but back in those days they terrorised the locals.

The settled districts ended around about the Clyde River area, where there were just a few huts, built by shepherds; tending sheep alone in the bush was the sort of job that appealed to ex-convicts. The bushrangers used to go out and knock off the odd sheep, which helped them survive. Pearce knew all about that way of life and it was what he and Greenhill were aiming for. Unfortunately, though, they were practically out of food. Desperation was setting in when they came across another Aboriginal camp. Again the two men managed to scare off the inhabitants and steal some food. They were safe for the moment, but Greenhill still jealously guarded the axe. Before long a horrible game of cat-and-mouse began; neither man was game enough to fall asleep.

As Pearce recorded in his confession:

We proceeded on travelling for a few days, continually watching each other, during which time he made several attempts to effect his purpose but I always guarded against such attempts and frustrated his design. One evening when he was asleep I crept slyly to the brush where he lay and took the axe from under his head, and gave him a severe blow on the head which deprived him of his life.

So Pearce was the last one to stay awake. From here on he was on his own. He was the only person who could tell the story. It took him an incredible seven weeks to walk out from Macquarie Harbour—an extraordinary feat of endurance. He travelled across the mountains, down into the centre of Tasmania, reaching the outer edge of European settlement at Shannon Hut, where he joined forces with a couple of bushrangers.

This motley lot shared the country with the Big River Tribe who still roamed around as they had for hundreds of years, hunting wallabies and wombats and gathering plants from the marshland. There's evidence, too, that they made use of a tree that's unique to the area. It's a subalpine tree called cider gum (*Eucalyptus gunnii)* and, as the name suggests, it's got a special characteristic. The sap of the tree is very sweet and tastes a bit like honey. When it ferments, it's intoxicating. Aboriginal people used to tap the trees and collect the sap in a hole at the foot of the trunk. Then they'd suck it through a reed or rolled bark. In fact, observers from the early days of settlement sometimes saw special corroborees being held around these trees.

Just sitting under a cider gum you really notice the smell—it's a bit like walking past a pub the morning after. Tastes a bit better, though—sweet and cidery. In fact, these days there's a commercial industry centred round these trees.

Well, back to Pearce and his bushranger mates, they were soon hunted down by the military, and in January 1823 they were ambushed in a stony gully at a place called Jericho. One of the fugitives was brought down with a volley of gunfire. Three and a half months after escaping from Sarah Island, Pearce was captured on the banks of the Jordan River.

You'll never guess what happened next. Alexander Pearce found himself back in

I imagine the magnificent scenery of Tasmania's south-west wilderness was lost on Alexander Pearce and his convict mates as they struggled towards the eastern settled districts and freedom back in 1822.

jail in Hobart Town. He confessed to everything, describing the murder and the cannibalism. But the magistrate wouldn't believe a thing. You see, there were no bodies—no evidence—so they reckoned Pearce was covering for his convict mates who were still on the run. What they did with him was they packed him up and sent him straight back to Macquarie Harbour, where he was forced to work in irons.

But the strange story of Alexander Pearce didn't finish there. Back at Sarah Island he became a bit of a hero amongst the other prisoners, who knew he'd broken out and made it back to the east. One of them, a young bloke by the name of Thomas Cox, hassled Pearce to break out again, and by mid-November Pearce had agreed. I guess Pearce could see a meal ticket in the young Thomas—literally.

But Pearce had learned at least one lesson—there was no way he was heading east again. Instead, the plan was to go north, towards the settlement at Port Dalrymple. They would stick to the coast where food was more plentiful. Unfortunately things didn't go according to plan, and yes, Pearce turned cannibal not too far up the track. But he was revolted by what he'd done and he signalled a passing schooner to come in and pick him up. He kept a piece of Cox's flesh to prove to the authorities that his story was true. All he really said in his own defence was, *No person can tell what he will do when driven by hunger.*

This time Pearce was believed and was sent to Hobart Town for trial. (Interestingly, the Supreme Court building where he was tried is still standing to this day.) By now Pearce had become a bit of a celebrity, and the local press recorded the details of his trial. It would have been a court reporter's dream, as this description from the *Hobart Town Gazette* shows:

Reports had associated the prisoner with cannibals, and recollecting as we did, the vampire legends of modern Greece, we confess that on this occasion our eyes glanced in fearfulness at the being who stood before a retributive judge, laden with the weight of human blood, and believed to have banqueted on human flesh.

Pearce was sentenced to death and went to the gallows on Monday 19 July, 1824.

It's a ghastly story all right—nightmare stuff. But I take my hat off to Alexander Pearce for the journey he made. After all, he was the first white man to cross Tasmania from west to east. And it was a long time before that journey was made again—

without the consumption of human flesh, I'll add! I guess it gives a whole new meaning to the words 'Ask your mates over for a barbeque'.

An interesting legend has grown up around Pearce that concerns a river on Tasmania's west coast called the Pieman. According to the legend, it was named after Alexander Pearce, a pastry maker convicted for selling 'unwholesome' pies in Hobart Town. What a tale! The truth is, the Pieman River was probably named after another convict—Thomas Kent, a baker who was known as 'The Pieman'—who escaped from Macquarie Harbour a few months after Pearce's second breakout. Kent was captured north of an unnamed river which became known as the Pieman.

But Pearce hasn't quite left us yet. After he'd been hanged and the artist had completed his death sketch, Pearce's body was sent off to the colonial hospital, where it was dissected. In due course the skull became part of a collection belonging to an American scientist, Dr Samuel Morton. These days Pearce's skull resides in a collection housed in the Department of Anthropology, University of Pennsylvania.

Ludwig Leichhardt

CHAPTER TWO

LUDWIG LEICHHARDT

I'LL ALWAYS REMEMBER my first trip to the Gilbert River in Queensland's Gulf country. At the time, I was a 12-year-old boy travelling with my parents. The Gilbert is fairly typical of the rivers in that country, and where we crossed it near Georgetown it had a wide flat sandy bed, with the occasional bit of water in it. I can't remember being aware then of just how the river got the name Gilbert, but within a few years I'd been told the story; since then it's meant so much more than just another Gulf river. That story goes back in time over 150 years, and the rather unlucky man who gave his name to the river was Mr John Gilbert, a naturalist accompanying Ludwig Leich-

hardt's expedition to Port Essington.

I'm going to come back to the Gilbert River incident a little later on, but first up I think it's worth having a look at the events that led to it. Ludwig Leichhardt's 1844–1845 journey of nearly 5000 kilometres from the Darling Downs, just west of Brisbane, to Port Essington, a small and remote settlement in the north-west corner of the Northern Territory, remains one of the most impressive accomplishments in the history of Australian exploration.

Over the years, many people have forgotten about Leichhardt's successful expedition and have focused instead on the mystery of his disappearance. That's fair enough, in a way; it's not every day that a party of seven men and 77 animals simply vanishes into thin air. That's what happened in 1848 after Leichhardt and his team had left from near the present day town of Roma, north-west of Brisbane, on a second attempt to reach the Swan River settlement on the west coast. They were never seen or heard from again. Almost a century and a half later we're really none the wiser as to what happened. But rather than speculating about Leichhardt's fate, I'd like to have a closer look at his Port Essington journey, because I reckon he was one of our best explorers.

Friedrich Wilhelm Ludwig Leichhardt was born in 1813 in the German state of Prussia. In those days before confederation, Prussia was Germany's most powerful state, and its strongly disciplined army was feared throughout Europe. Young Leichhardt did pretty well at school and went on to pursue university studies in Berlin and Göttingen, where he met the Nicholson brothers, a couple of English students, with whom he forged a strong friendship. In 1837, after studying science and medicine for a few years, Leichhardt accompanied William Nicholson back to England. For the next four years the two men travelled through England and parts of Europe, continuing their medical and scientific studies.

Around this time Leichhardt should have served a term in the Prussian army, but he had no interest in doing that, so he carefully avoided returning to Germany. Instead he focused on becoming a scientific explorer, and he chose Australia (or New Holland as it was known in those days) as the place to live out this dream. *The interior, the heart of this dark continent, is my goal, and I will never relinquish the quest for it until I get there,* he wrote. Nicholson, who had been Leichhardt's benefactor during their years of travelling, shouted Leichhardt his fare to Australia, and the two parted ways.

Shortly after arriving in Sydney in 1842, Leichhardt presented himself (along with a letter of introduction) to Sir Thomas Mitchell, Surveyor-General of New South Wales. Nobody else in Australia could match Leichhardt's academic and practical scientific background; he was qualified for field research in zoology, botany, geography, geology and meteorology. Mitchell was impressed and agreed to take Leichhardt along as naturalist on his next exploring expedition.

Since the 1830s, the trading merchants and graziers had been putting pressure on the government to open up the country around the northern end of Australia. The

We stood with our whole train on the brink of a deep precipice, of perhaps 1800 feet descent, *Leichhardt wrote of his first encounter with Kakadu landscape. It took them a few days to find a way down to the bottom.* Our horses and cattle were, however, in a distressing condition. The passage along rocky creeks, between the loose blocks of which their feet were constantly slipping, had rendered them very foot-sore, and had covered their legs with sores.

*The Roper River is a great
environment for bush tucker. It
has barra, yabbies and plenty of
bird life too.*

British had already made three attempts at establishing a presence up north: Fort Dundas on Melville Island in 1824, Fort Wellington at Raffles Bay on the Cobourg Peninsula in 1827, and finally at Port Essington in 1840. The settlements at Forts Dundas and Wellington had lasted about two years each, but Port Essington seemed a better bet. There were two main reasons for these outposts of civilisation: they were a warning to the French who'd been nosing around the northern coastline; and they were there in the hope of setting up a trading port with Singapore, India and the 'spice islands' (or Indonesia, as they're now called).

What the merchants and graziers wanted was an overland route to connect the eastern seaboard ports with Port Essington. You see, to travel there by sea required finding a way through the maze of coral in the Great Barrier Reef, then through Torres Strait and around the top of Australia—a long and hazardous journey. (Mind you, the overland route wouldn't have been much better, but that was what they wanted at the time.)

Back in those days, Mitchell believed in the existence of a great river flowing north that could be followed to its mouth, thus providing a relatively easy route to the coast. However, it would take some time to organise an expedition to find it. For a few months Leichhardt worked as a private tutor, but his heart was set on learning as much as possible about the Australian bush. During the next two years, he travelled to the Hunter River area, New England, Moreton Bay and the Darling Downs. He usually went alone on horseback, collecting all sorts of specimens as he studied Australian natural history in the field. He also made close studies of any Aboriginal people he came across, and was keen to learn as much as he could about their food, habits and customs. While some colonists regarded the lone traveller as a bit of an eccentric, most of the graziers showered this enthusiastic, inquisitive visitor with outback hospitality. Amongst these generous souls were the Archer brothers of Moreton Bay; they helped to inspire Leichhardt with the idea of looking for new grazing country to the north.

Back in Sydney, as Sir Thomas Mitchell was still awaiting approval from Britain and local government funding for his proposed overland journey to Port Essington, Leichhardt jumped in and organised his own privately funded expedition. Businessmen and graziers coughed up enough money, equipment and animals to allow Leichhardt to put his plan into action—private enterprise at work.

He reckoned that seven months would see him and his party in Port Essington, so he stocked up accordingly. At the end of September 1844, ten men, 16 bullocks, 17 horses and a couple of dogs departed from a property near the Darling Downs *launched, buoyant with hope, into the wilderness of Australia, winding our way round the first rise beyond the station, with a full chorus of 'God Save the Queen'*. Provisions included 1200 pounds of flour, 200 pounds of sugar, 80 pounds of tea and 20 pounds of gelatine. Leichhardt advised his party of volunteers to provide themselves with two strong pairs of trousers, three strong shirts, and two pairs of shoes. Some also took ponchos made of calico soaked in oil to keep out the rain.

Leichhardt's expedition members James Calvert (left), John Murphy (centre) and John Roper (right) many years after their 1844–45 journey to Port Essington.

Most of Leichhardt's men were very young: John Murphy, 15 years old and James Calvert, 19, had travelled to Australia on the same ship as Leichhardt; John Roper, who had recently arrived in Sydney, was 24; Leichhardt himself was 31 years old. John Gilbert, who had worked as a collector for the famous birdo, John Gould, was older than the others. William Phillips, a ticket-of-leave convict, and Harry Brown, an Aborigine from the Newcastle district, also started with the party from Sydney.

In Brisbane three more men joined up: Pemberton Hodgson, a local squatter; Caleb, an American negro; and another Aborigine, Charley Fisher. Charley was the real character on the expedition, and we'll catch up with him a bit later on.

It took some time for the men and bullocks to get acquainted. Apart from carrying loads, the bullocks went along to provide meat for the expeditioners. Loading the animals each morning was a bit of a job, and when they first started it used to take a couple of hours. As often as not, the bullocks would throw their loads; Leichhardt would take the necessary time to repair any damage done to the packsaddles and straps.

The first two months of the expedition were a good shake-down period. By early November Leichhardt knew that his provisions weren't going to hold out, so Hodgson and Caleb turned back. Before leaving, they helped kill the first bullock, cutting the meat into thin slices and drying it in the sun. *This, our first experiment—on the favourable result of which the success of our expedition entirely depended—kept us, during the process, in a state of great excitement*, Leichhardt recorded. *It succeeded, however, to our great joy, and inspired us with confidence for the future*. The small bullock yielded 65 pounds of meat and 15 of fat. Leichhardt was a great improviser who wasted nothing, and he used some of the fat to rub into the leather harnesses and saddles.

With the party reduced to eight men, daily rations were fixed at six pounds of flour and three of dried meat. As Leichhardt had no deadlines or schedules to keep to, he could afford the luxury of time to make detailed scientific observations and send Brown and Charley out to hunt animals and gather bush tucker. Both of the men were good shots, and John Gilbert wasn't bad either, having had plenty of practice shooting birds for Gould's collection. Mind you, Charley was a bit cheeky, and this caused Leichhardt to sack him on one occasion—only to give him his job back the next day, of course.

Leichhardt's decision to travel as lightly as possible, with a small, highly mobile team, shows that he was ahead of his time as an explorer of outback Australia. He chose to be self-reliant too, rather than trying to link up with supply ships along the coast. His journal records the expedition's day-to-day progress and provides a fascinating account of the geology, natural history and Aboriginal occupation of the country they traversed.

There's no doubt that Leichhardt was a skilled bushman, as this description of looking for water indicates:

my search was first made in the neighbourhood of hills, ridges and ranges, which from their extent and elevation were most likely to lead me to it, either in beds of creeks, or rivers,

or in water-holes, parallel to them. In an open country, there are many indications which a practised eye will readily seize: a cluster of trees of a greener foliage, hollows with luxuriant grass, eagles circling in the air, crows, cockatoos, pigeons (especially before sunset), and the call of Grallina australis *and flocks of little finches, would always attract our attention.*

For the first stage of the journey, Leichhardt followed the Queensland coast at an average distance of 240 kilometres inland, discovering jagged peaks, rugged mountains, lush valleys and untold acres of grazing land. He also discovered the *particularly striking and imposing* Expedition Range, important rivers (including the Suttor, Dawson, Mackenzie and Burdekin), and plenty of smaller rivers, creeks and ranges. As Leichhardt was keen to thank the people who had helped him get his expedition on the road, he named geographical features after them. He honoured his expedition members in the same way, which is quite a contrast to some of the 'government' explorers who tended to use names from royalty and government around the bush.

In one of the many lectures he gave on his return to Sydney, Leichhardt reckoned he could divide his line of travel into eight different sections. It's probably worth having a look at those now, to gain a better understanding of the country that lay ahead of the men:

Cape York Peninsula's wet season generally lasts from December to April. Rivers break their banks and flood over the surrounding plains inundating the whole area.

1 Scrubby sandstone country between the Darling Downs and Peak Range, including the Dawson and Mackenzie Rivers. The discovery of coal in this region reminded Leichhardt of the Hunter River area;

2 The basalt plains and open forests of Peak Range, including the Isacks and Upper Suttor Rivers;

3 Limestone country of the Lower Suttor and Burdekin Rivers, with lagoons, deep creeks and mountain ranges;

4 The Lynd and Mitchell Rivers and the eastern coast of the Gulf of Carpentaria—open forests and grassy plains, mostly clayey ironstone;

5 The 'Plains of Promise', named by Captain Stokes, where the Flinders, Albert and Nicholson Rivers flow into the Gulf of Carpentaria;

6 The scrubby west coast of the Gulf with the Van Alphen, the Abel Tasman, the Seven Emu, Robinson, Macarthur, Limmen Bight and Wickham Rivers—predominantly large saltwater rivers, dense tea-tree scrub and stringy-bark forests;

7 The Roper River and Arnhem Land—open, well-grassed country interspersed with sandstone ridges;

8 The Alligator River and the Cobourg Peninsula—large swampy lagoons, extensive plains and densely forested ironstone ridges.

In his journal, Leichhardt describes a typical day in the life of the expedition:

I usually rise when I hear the merry laugh of the laughing-jackass . . . a loud cooee then rouses my companions—Brown to make tea, Mr Calvert to season the stew with salt and marjoram, and myself and the others to wash, and to prepare our breakfast, which, for the party, consists of two pounds and a-half of meat, stewed over night; and to each a quart pot of tea. Mr Calvert then gives to each his portion, and, by the time this important duty is performed, Charley generally arrives with the horses, which are then prepared for their day's duty.

After breakfast, Charley goes with John Murphy to fetch the bullocks, which are generally brought in a little after seven o'clock a.m. . . . at about a quarter to eight o'clock, we move on, and continue travelling four hours, and, if possible, select a spot for our camp.

. . . as soon as the camp is pitched, and the horses and bullocks unloaded, we have all our allotted duties; to make the fire falls to my share; Brown's duty is to fetch water for tea; and Mr Calvert weighs out a pound and a-half of flour for a fat cake, which is enjoyed more than any other meal; the large teapot being empty, Mr Calvert weighs out two and a-half pounds of dry meat to be stewed for our late dinner; and, during the afternoon, everyone follows his own pursuits, such as washing and mending clothes, repairing saddles, pack-saddles, and packs; my occupation is to write my log, and lay down my

*route, or make an excursion in the vicinity of the camp to botanize etc. or ride out
reconnoitring.*

*My companions also write down their remarks, and wander about gathering seeds,
or looking for curious pebbles. Mr Gilbert takes his gun to shoot birds. A loud cooee again
unites us towards sunset round our table cloth; and, whilst enjoying our meals, the subject
of the day's journey, the past, the present, and the future, by turns engage our attention,
or furnish matter for conversation and remark, according to the respective humour of the
parties.*

Leichhardt appears to have really loved the Australian bush—he felt at home
there and took great delight in every new discovery he made of a plant or an animal.
His journal is full of these descriptions. He had an open, inquiring mind and this really
stood him in good stead for surviving the hardships of outback life.

Leichhardt also made a habit of going into deserted Aboriginal camps to study
food preparation and other customs:

*Three koolimans (vessels of stringy bark) were full of honey water, from one of which I
took a hearty draught, and left a brass button for payment. Dillis, fish spears, a roasted
bandicoot, a species of potato, wax, a bundle of tea-tree bark with dry shavings; several
flints fastened with human hair to the ends of sticks, and which are used as knives to cut
their skin and food; a spindle to make strings of opossum wool; and several other small
utensils, were in their camp.*

Of course these camps were deserted, no doubt because of Leichhardt and his
party's sudden arrival on the scene. I can't help but wonder what he expected the
Aborigines to do with the brass button.

For me, it's the last part of the journey, from the Gulf of Carpentaria through to
Port Essington, that's by far the most interesting. Because of the rugged nature of the
country and their dwindling supplies, it was also the most challenging time for them.

These days Queensland's Gulf country is mostly taken up by huge cattle properties—
exactly what the graziers of Leichhardt's day had wanted. Nowadays, some of these
properties take in tourists to help subsidise their incomes. There are all sorts of things
to do in that part of the world; fishing and birdwatching are probably two of the most

popular pastimes. I love to get up there whenever I can to recharge my batteries, and I don't mind the odd bit of barra fishing myself. It was on one of these cattle properties—Rutland Plains station—that John Gilbert met his end. On June 28 1845, the men arrived at a chain of shallow lagoons surrounded by a belt of tea-trees, and decided to make camp there. They organised their camp, as Leichhardt described:

Mr Roper and Mr Calvert made their tent within the belt of trees, with its opening towards the packs; whilst Mr Gilbert and Murphy constructed theirs amongst the little trees, with its entrance from the camp. Mr Phillips's was, as usual, far from the others, and at the opposite side of the water. Our fire place was made outside of the trees, on the banks.

Some time after seven o'clock most of the men had gone to bed for the night and Leichhardt was dozing near the fire when he was woken up by calls for help. Apparently the local Aborigines had put in a surprise attack, showering spears on the tents of Roper, Calvert, Gilbert and Murphy. They also threw some at Phillips's tent and a few more towards the fire.

Over the years there's been a whole bunch of speculation as to the reason for this attack, resulting in a couple of possible answers. One suggestion is that the explorers had, that afternoon, unwittingly stumbled across a sacred ceremonial ground. Another possibility is that some of Leichhardt's men had been fooling around with the local women. We'll probably never be sure of the reason for the attack, but there's little doubt that it was provoked. It's interesting to note that, at the very start of the expedition, Leichhardt insisted that the men keep watch at night. But up till this time there'd been no real trouble with the Aborigines, so the idea of running a night watch had fallen by the wayside.

Anyway, Roper and Calvert sustained spear wounds and Gilbert dropped down dead. In the confusion, Murphy managed to escape from his tent and hide behind a tree, opening fire on the Aborigines. The men put out their fire and *passed an anxious night, in a state of most painful suspense as to the fate of our still surviving companions.*

Next morning, Leichhardt inspected the injuries more closely.

Mr Roper had received two or three spear wounds in the scalp of his head; one spear had passed through his left arm, another into his cheek below the jugal [sic] bone, and penetrated the orbit, and injured the optic nerve, and another in his loins, besides a heavy blow on the shoulder. Mr Calvert had received several severe blows from a waddi; one on the nose which had crushed the nasal bones; one on the elbow, and another on the back of his hand; besides which, a barbed spear had entered his groin; and another into his knee. As may be readily imagined, both suffered great pain, and were scarcely able to move.

I bet the men were glad of Leichhardt's medical knowledge, which undoubtedly saved their wounds from infection. The thing that amazes me is the fact that not only did these young men survive their wounds, but they also continued their journey—very, very gutsy stuff.

As for the dead man, *The spear that terminated poor Gilbert's existence, had entered the chest, between the clavicle and the neck; but made so small a wound, that, for some time, I was unable to detect it.*

That afternoon they buried Gilbert in a shallow grave. Leichhardt read a funeral service and afterwards, fearing the Aborigines might dig up the body, they lit a big fire over the grave.

At the start of his 1844–45 expedition, Leichhardt had insisted that the men keep watch at night. As they had no real trouble during the first stage of their journey, the idea of running a night watch fell by the wayside. Then on June 28, 1845, some time after 7.00 pm, the local Aboriginals put in a surprise attack.

Leichhardt had the good sense to realise they weren't welcome in that neck of the woods. On 30 June, with Roper and Calvert still in agony, they made tracks:

All our energies were roused, we found ourselves in danger, and, as was absolutely necessary, we strained every nerve to extricate ourselves from it: but I was well aware, that the more coolly we went to work, the better we should succeed.

With supplies diminishing and Port Essington still a long way off, the men relied more and more on the skills of Charley and Brown in finding tucker. All sorts of birds went into the pot: emus, ibis, ducks, bustards and even a pelican. They'd run out of salt back down the track, but now they came across a whole heap of it just lying on the ground, and you can still find salt in the Gulf country even today. It comes in with the high Gulf tides right up to the creeks and estuaries, and then the tide goes out, leaving small ponds of salty water to dry out, which it does, leaving a thick salty crust behind.

The first settlers in the area around Escott station used the same salt patches as Leichhardt did to gather salt. Apparently the explorers were able to collect enough to last the remainder of the journey, which doesn't surprise me, as there's stacks of it lying around the place. Not surprisingly, they also met up with more and more Aboriginal people, as the Gulf country is so rich in bush tucker that it's a bit like a supermarket in its own way.

One of the things Leichhardt noted through this country was the number of grass fires that had been deliberately lit by the local Aboriginal people. But he also twigged as to the reason:

It is no doubt connected with a systematic management of their runs, to attract game to particular spots . . . The natives frequently burn the high and stiff grass, particularly along shady creeks, with the intention of driving the concealed game out of it; and we have frequently seen them watching anxiously, even for lizards, when other game was wanting.

By early September, as they slowly made their way up the west coast of the Gulf of Carpentaria, only five of the original 16 bullocks were left. Here and there the men passed Aboriginal fish traps, built from sticks across narrow parts of tidal rivers and streams. Leichhardt also finally worked out how to eat the fruit of the pandanus without suffering:

I frequently tasted the fine-looking fruit of the Pandanus, but was every time severely punished with sore lips and a blistered tongue; and the first time that I ate it, I was attacked by a violent diarrhoea. I could not make out how the natives neutralized the noxious properties of the fruit; which, from the large heaps in their camps, seemed to form no small portion of their food. The fruit appeared either to have been soaked, or roasted and broken, to obtain the kernels; for which purpose we invariably found large flat stones and pebbles to pound them with. I supposed that they washed out the sweet mealy matter contained between the stringy fibres . . . I, consequently, gathered some very ripe fruit, scraped the soft part with a knife, and washed it until all the sweet substance was out, and then boiled it; by which process it lost all its sharpness, had a very pleasant taste, and, taken in moderate quantities, did not affect the bowels. The fruit should be so ripe as to be ready to drop from the trees.

Ludwig Leichhardt recorded in his journal, I frequently tasted the fine-looking fruit of the Pandanus, but was every time severely punished with sore lips and a blistered tongue. Leichhardt, a keen botanist, actually learned a lot about bush tucker from his observations of Aboriginal practices and was pretty chuffed when he finally cracked the secret of preparing the pandanus fruit.

By mid-September the small party must have looked pretty sad and sorry. Their shirts and trousers were patched in places and threadbare in others; luckily they'd had the foresight to take better care of their shoes. Game was not so plentiful, and the bullocks were showing signs of the long, hard journey. The men drank the last of their tea and, with Prussian frugality, Leichhardt now added dried bullock skin to their soup at night. They made a coffee substitute from the *bean of the Mackenzie*, which they drank right down to the grounds. Phillips in particular was very fond of his brew, and was always on the look-out for possible coffee substitutes. Now I don't know this 'Mackenzie bean' that Leichhardt refers to, but I half suspect that it may be one of the *Brachiton* species, which can be used after being roasted and ground up to form a rough substitute for coffee. I've tried it myself a couple of times, but it helps to have a good imagination.

A month later Leichhardt named the Four Archers, four flat-topped sandstone peaks, in honour of the Archer brothers of Moreton Bay, who had encouraged him to look for new grazing land. These four flat-topped hills are almost right beside the road as you travel toward the Roper River after crossing the Limmen. In fact you can take a little side-track into them at the boundary of Nathan River station. The small one

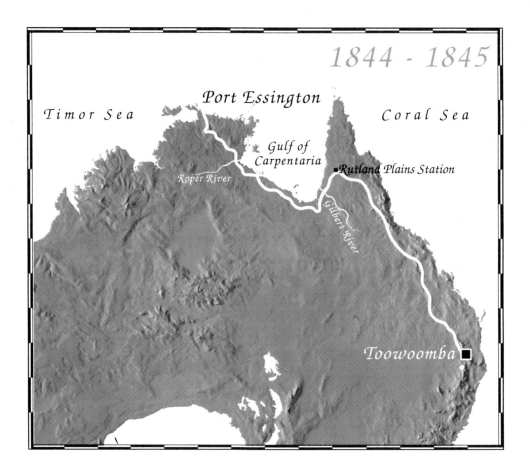

right next to the Limmen is the one Leichhardt climbed to find a way to get his party across the water, and just as well he did. There are plenty of crocodiles in this water, and from the top of that hill he saw a small rock bar leading to the northern bank, which was just what he was looking for. The explorers were now getting really close to the country that I love best.

A few days later, the only surviving dog died. He'd been a great help in hunting game, and besides that, Leichhardt was really fond of him, and he was pretty cut up. To make things worse (but probably thinking he was doing the right thing considering the death of the dog) Brown started humming the soldier's death march. According to Leichhardt, this *had such a singularly depressing effect on my feelings, that I was frequently constrained to request him to change his tune.*

On 19 October Leichhardt named the Roper River in honour of his team-mate, John Roper, who was the first to see it. The Roper is one of the most impressive rivers in northern Australia (and we do have some good ones). It runs for hundreds of kilometres, gradually turning from salt to fresh water. I can tell you I've put down my swag in Roper country on more than one occasion. Of course it has all the usual attractions, like barra, yabbies, crocodiles, and (in days past) buffalo as well. In fact, there's still the occasional old buff roaming around the Roper if you know where to look. The banks are invariably lined with giant paperbark trees, which offer excellent shade during the heat of the day, but above all, the Roper has a peacefulness that I feel is on its own. Nothing beats floating down the Roper in a small boat, just drifting under the overhanging branches of the *Pandanus* and *Melaleuca* trees. Of course there's

Aboriginal guides Charley Fisher (left) and Harry Brown (right) were the real heroes of Leichhardt's expedition. His team would not have survived their journey to Port Essington without the hunting and food gathering skills of these two men.

plenty of bird life around the place too, and that was probably just as well.

Finding game was now much easier for Charley and Brown:

we had fifty-one ducks and two geese for the three meals; and they were all eaten, with the exception of a few bony remains, which some of the party carried to the next camp.

Crossing the Roper, however, proved to be a major challenge. For a day or so they moved along the south bank looking for the best place to get across, and then Charley brought Leichhardt the disastrous news that three of the horses had drowned. Leichhardt was absolutely devastated. The few remaining bullocks were so weak they were unable to carry any more loads, so the loss of the horses meant that Leichhardt would have to ditch the bulk of his botanical collection.

The fruit of many a day's work was consigned to the fire; and tears were in my eyes when I saw one of the most interesting results of my expedition vanish into smoke.

Soon, Aborigines attracted the explorers' attention from the northern banks of the river. Next morning they crossed over to Leichhardt's side, and a friendly exchange of presents followed. Leichhardt gave them horse nails, which the Aborigines asked him to bend into fish hooks. Leichhardt recorded, *They had doubtless seen or heard of white people before; but of our horses and bullocks they were much afraid, and asked me whether they could bite.*

Eventually the men found the Roper River bar crossing, a natural rock formation that stretches from one bank to the other. Nowadays a cement causeway has been built on top of the rocks to support the vehicle traffic, but this causeway is continuously covered with fresh running water and, along with the green vegetation, forms a beautiful sight. Sadly, the scene is no longer as picturesque as it once was (thanks to the rubbish and beer cans in particular), and for this we can't blame the visitor or tourist—it's all been done by the locals.

Anyway, Leichhardt and his men walked their horses and bullocks across the rocky bar to the Roper's northern bank. By now the men and animals were very weak and nearly at the end of their tethers. Then at the junction of the Wilton and Roper Rivers, another horse drowned, leaving just nine.

The site of the drowning is now Urapunga country, and over the years I've spent many a night camped on the wide verandah of the Urapunga homestead, or the 'Wilton Hilton' as it was often called. A mate of mine, Ray Fryer, used to own it then, but no more. The homestead was located only a few hundred metres from these two great rivers. For me, it was a sort of rest stop after I'd been on the track for a couple of months, and a chance to take a few days off, and perhaps catch a fish or two. I have a lot of good memories of those days.

But there was no rest for Leichhardt and his men. From time to time, the men supplemented their rations with the odd flying fox, whenever Charley or Brown could shoot them. One afternoon at the end of October, the two men returned to camp with 30, leaving another 50 hanging wounded in the trees. While they were out,

By the time Leichhardt and his men got to the Top End they'd been on the road for the better part of a year and they were running very low on supplies. Luckily this area is rich in game, including flocks of magpie geese, which helped keep the men alive. Charley and Brown were often despatched with the shotgun to shoot birds and mammals for the pot.

Charley reckoned he'd seen a strange animal with two horns in a waterhole. As Brown saw a crocodile in the same waterhole on the following day, Leichardt dismissed Charley's horned beast as a crocodile with imaginary horns.

Well, I don't agree with Leichhardt on that one. I reckon Charley did see a horned animal—in fact I think what he saw was a water buffalo with just its head sticking up above the surface of the water. You see, when Fort Dundas was established back in the 1820s, it had been stocked with all sorts of animals, including the Asiatic water buffalo, *Bubalus bubalis*. When Fort Dundas was abandoned in favour of the new settlement (Fort Wellington at Raffles Bay) the people and livestock were transferred across. Then when Fort Wellington failed, most of the animals were simply left behind. By 1845, when Leichhardt and his men were roaming across the Top End, the buffalo had been on the loose for about 15 years, giving them plenty of time to spread out.

Leichhardt's camps were very well organised, as this lithograph of his camp at Dried Beef Creek shows. He was a great improviser who wasted nothing. Whenever they stopped to kill a bullock, the meat was cut into thin strips and dried in the sun; the fat was used to grease the leather harnesses and saddles.

In fact it's been estimated that they had spread well past the Roper River by the time Leichhardt and his mob came through.

By November the weather was really getting hot and the bullocks took any chance they could to cool down with a refreshing swim. Unfortunately, one of them, as Leichhardt recorded,

> that which carried the remainder of my botanical collection—watched his opportunity, and plunged into a deep pond, where he was quietly swimming about and enjoying himself, whilst I was almost crying with vexation at seeing all my plants thoroughly soaked.

Migratory birds, wallabies, kangaroos and all sorts of bush tucker were in plentiful supply. In mid-November they passed a huge roost of flying foxes;

> suspended in thick clusters on the highest trees in the most shady and rather moist parts of the valley. They started as we passed, and the flapping of their large membranous wings produced a sound like that of a hail-storm.

Charley and Brown shot 67 flying foxes, bringing 55 into camp to be distributed among the crew.

I'll tell you a bit about these flying foxes. They're not the blood-sucking varieties that nightmares are made of; these mammals like to feed on fruit or the blossom of eucalypts and other native trees, and they act as pollinators and dispersers of seeds. In fact many of the fruit-bearing trees of the tropics rely primarily on these animals to spread their seeds. Large colonies of flying foxes, such as Leichhardt described, are increasingly rare these days, partly because their habitat's been destroyed, although they still tend to pop up around the place from time to time. When they take off at dusk, they simply blacken out the sky. I remember one time up in the Territory only a couple of years ago, I was driving along not far from the Roper River and I started to pass under a colony of flying foxes as they flew overhead. They just covered the sky from one horizon to another. Well, I drove on and on, and still they kept coming, thousands and thousands of them, and that continued for a full 15 kilometres.

On 17 November Leichhardt and his party reached the Arnhem Land escarpment, so I suppose you could say that they were the first white tourists to pass through what

Imagine trying to get horses, carts and 100 sheep through this country. That's exactly what Kennedy and his men did in 1848 as they struggled from the coast up to the Atherton Tableland.

This is typical of the rainforest country Kennedy tried to take on around his landing point on the Hull River.

Woody supports, called buttress
roots, grow from the trunks of a
number of Australian tropical
rainforest trees. Buttress roots
were used by rainforest
Aboriginal people to make
fighting shields.

is now Kakadu national park. *We stood with our whole train on the brink of a deep precipice, of perhaps 1800 feet descent.* It took them a few days to find a way down to the bottom. *Our horses and cattle were, however, in a distressing condition. The passage along rocky creeks, between the loose blocks of which their feet were constantly slipping, had rendered them very foot-sore, and had covered their legs with sores.*

The wet season had started, and every day or so the men, animals and few remaining supplies were drenched. This really caused problems when they slaughtered one of the remaining bullocks and tried to dry the meat: *its soft state enabled the maggots to nestle in it; and the rain to which it had been exposed, rendered it very insipid.*

When I first read Leichhardt's journal, I found the answer to a question that had been nagging me for a long time. I've always wondered why, in the middle of the Northern Territory, there's a creek called Snowdrop. As it turns out, it was named after one of the bullocks—he had a little white dot on his forehead.

Heavy rain brought flies and mosquitoes and also turned the ground into a bog. The men continued to bump into mobs of Aborigines, but had no further trouble with them. The usual course of action was an attempt at communication, followed by a friendly exchange of presents. Fortunately there was plenty of water and increasingly large amounts of game. In fact, the closer the men got to their destination, the more interest the Aborigines showed in them, and the more helpful they became.

Water lilies (Nymphaea sp.) thrive in the billabongs of northern Australia. The bulbs and young shoots of most of these beautiful plants are edible.

Imagine the expeditioners' surprise when, one early December morning, they encountered an Aboriginal man who spoke English: *we heard him utter distinctly the words, 'Commandant!' 'come here!!' 'very good!!!' 'what's your name?!!!!'* Leichhardt and his men were so thrilled, they showered the man and his companion with presents, receiving in return bunches of goose feathers, which the Aborigines used to brush away flies.

These Aboriginal men knew all about the Port Essington outpost, and Leichhardt hoped they might guide his party to their destination. It was not to be, but they and some others of their 200-strong tribe brought food to the explorers and also showed them where to find water. In complete contrast to the explorers, these Aborigines were in excellent condition, and according to Leichhardt they wouldn't eat the meat or green hide offered to them:

they took it, but could not overcome their repugnance, and tried to drop it without being seen by us. Poor fellows! They did not know how gladly we should have received it back! They were the stoutest and fattest men we had met.

The expedition continued on its way, with more friendly Aborigines showing the men the best place to cross the East Alligator River. Charley and Brown shot more flying foxes, along with waterfowl, including the magpie geese that inhabit the swamps and floodplains of this wetland country.

The old camps of the natives, which we passed in the forest, were strewed with the shells of goose eggs, which shewed what an important article these birds formed in the culinary department of the natives; and, whilst their meat and eggs served them for food, their feathers afforded them a protection against the flies which swarmed round their bodies during the day.

Most of the men had boils, which Leichhardt reckoned were caused by a want of cleanliness. More likely it was a result of poor nutrition as well as the tropical climate encouraging infection of every scratch and hair follicle. But once again his medical knowledge stood them in good stead, and by lancing the boils he saved the men a lot of pain further down the track.

Before long the men came across more friendly tribes of Aborigines, some of whom spoke a smattering of English. They were now about a week away from Port Essington, and in the nick of time the last bullock's life was spared when Brown shot a wild buffalo. They shared the meat with their Aboriginal friends, who stayed to guide them through the maze of billabongs that now confronted them. By this time the party had been away from civilisation for 15 months and was presumed lost or dead.

I've been to Port Essington several times and it never ceases to amaze me. You can drive to Cobourg Peninsula easily enough, and there you can camp for a bit. But to get across water to the remains of the old settlement you'll have to get hold of a decent boat. I might add that to drive into Cobourg you also have to get a permit, but that's no great problem. It's incredible to think that after all the effort that was put in to getting Port Essington up and running it was closed down after just 11 years. In the end, disease, poor nutrition and enormous hardship, combined with isolation,

got the better of the inhabitants. You can still see a few reminders of the old

establishment. They used a lot of local rock and lime to build a number of the structures

and their foundations, so all of those bits and pieces are there to have a good look at,

including the local hospital and cottage chimneys, and of course the lime kiln itself.

These hand-made Cornish chimneys are all that remain of the houses built by the British at Victoria settlement. They look right out of place in the tropics; mad dogs and Englishmen were alive and well in those days!

Finally, on 17 December 1845, Ludwig Leichhardt and his men staggered in to

Port Essington, where the local Commandant, Captain Macarthur, and his officers

were both surprised and delighted to see them. Leichhardt wrote of the experience, *I

was deeply affected in finding myself again in civilized society, and could scarcely speak, the

words growing big with tears and emotion.*

The explorers stayed at the settlement for a month while they waited for a ship

to take them back to Sydney. They'd covered an incredible 4800 kilometres of

unexplored country with the loss of only one man, and you really have to be impressed

by this whole expedition. But for me, Charley Fisher was the hero of the story. He

was a real character, and he and Brown kept the men alive with their contributions

of bush tucker, without which I seriously doubt they would have arrived at Port

Essington at all.

Based on past experiences,
Kennedy figured he'd need 28
horses and three carts to manage
the provisions and equipment.
Little did he know the gear that
worked in the back blocks of
western NSW just wasn't suited
to the Cape York landscape.

CHAPTER THREE

KENNEDY AND JACKY

THE RATHER TRAGIC story of the explorer, Edmund Besley Court Kennedy, has been with me for almost as long as I can remember. I suppose it really started back in primary school in North Queensland when, as a young schoolboy, I was flicking through the Social Studies textbook. Suddenly I came across a really dramatic sketch of a man who'd been speared. He was slumped forward, his gun falling to the ground, and the barb of the spear sticking through the front of his chest. Not only that, but the sketch showed he was in the middle of a thick jungle—the whole scene depicted a real Boys' Own adventure.

The image of the speared explorer made a real

impression on me, and I was fascinated by the story that went with it. But that was just the beginning, because some years later he was waiting for me at boarding school on the Atherton Tableland. The school's two houses—Leichhardt and Kennedy—were named after explorers who'd passed through the local area. Needless to say, I was allocated to Kennedy house.

As events turned out, about ten years later I found myself involved in an unusual exercise with a small group of young soldiers. We were searching the mangrove banks of the Escape River, near the tip of Cape York, in an attempt to find the place where Kennedy had been speared. Luckily we had with us a copy of Captain Simpson's description, written when he accompanied the first party that tried to find the unfortunate explorer's body, back in the late 1840s.

Even now, twenty odd years later, I can vividly recall our anticipation as we moved along the Escape's southern bank looking for a creek that joined the main river system. Suddenly we found it, and after following it for a few hundred yards we broke through the thick scrub to see a large, open plain. This was exactly what we'd hoped to find: the broad wetland area on which Kennedy had been speared. As far as we knew at the time, we were the first European people to tread that ground since Captain Simpson and his rescue party.

I reckon it was near this site where the explorer Edmund Kennedy was speared. Back in 1848 there were three of these giant termite mounds on the broad wetland area adjacent to the Escape River, but these days there's just one left standing.

The plain where Kennedy died was a far cry from the thick jungle of the artist's imagination, but this was my first experience of 'hands on' exploration and I felt as though I was unearthing history. Unbeknownst to me, this was just the first of many historical retracings I would make, and my involvement with Mr Kennedy was far from over. But who was this man, and why did he die so tragically in such a remote part of the Australian continent?

Kennedy was born in 1818 on the Channel island of Guernsey. His father was a colonel and war veteran who, with his wife, raised a close-knit, religious family of six children. Rather than following his father into an army career, Kennedy opted for commerce. When he was in his late teens he went to work in Brazil, but the company that employed him went bankrupt, and in 1838 he moved to London. There he bumped into a friend of his father's, a marine surveyor named Charles James Tyers, who was about to leave for northern Australia. Tyers was to be involved in setting up a British outpost at Port Essington, and he promised to let Colonel Kennedy know if there was any future for young men in Australia.

Later that year, news came back that young Kennedy could secure himself a position in the Surveyor-General's Department in Sydney, if he passed the obligatory entrance exam. Kennedy was pretty excited about this idea, and enrolled in a 'Practical Surveying and Levelling' class in a London college. He showed a natural aptitude for surveying and really enjoyed it. By the end of 1839, Edmund Besley Court Kennedy was on a ship bound for New South Wales.

He arrived in Sydney in 1840, and thanks to the many letters of introduction from his father he was welcomed into the local social scene. After passing the entrance exam Kennedy was quickly appointed to the position of assistant surveyor, with a pretty good salary. His first job was to go out and survey the country around Portland Bay, part of the 'Australia Felix' pastoral land that had recently been discovered by Sir Thomas Mitchell, the Surveyor-General of New South Wales. This area was way down south, near the South Australian border.

Kennedy was now just 22 years old and pretty happy about his new position. Life in the Australian bush was challenging and very different from anything he'd yet experienced: his assistants were all convicts, fresh food was in short supply, the work was hard and equipment not quite up to scratch. Of his early encounters with the local Aborigines he wrote, *they have been very troublesome lately in every part of the Colony and I sincerely trust they will soon be exterminated.* That gives us a bit of an indication of things to come.

During the few years he spent in the Portland Bay area, Kennedy gained a lot of valuable surveying experience and proved himself a good and popular leader. Apparently he was a bit of a Flash Harry around town as well, and was welcomed in the social circles (such as they were) of the outback. He enjoyed life in the bush, had a strong sense of commitment to duty, and was a sincere, hard worker. Back in Sydney, glowing reports of his efforts really impressed his boss, Sir Thomas Mitchell, whom he was yet to meet.

In 1843, with a wealth of experience and adventure under his belt, Kennedy returned to Sydney. By this time Mitchell was obsessed with finding an overland route to Port Essington and, along the way, solving the mystery of the river systems to the north-west of the settled districts. He was convinced that an investigation of this area would lead to the discovery of a mighty river like the Murray-Darling that flowed into the Gulf of Carpentaria. Approval and funding for the venture were slow to come, but when they did Mitchell unexpectedly appointed Kennedy second-in-command.

At the end of 1845 Mitchell, Kennedy and their team set off, crossing the Macquarie and Barwon Rivers north-west of Sydney. On reaching the Condamine River, they learned that the explorer Ludwig Leichhardt had succeeded in finding a route to Port Essington. Mitchell continued north, still hoping to discover his 'big river'.

The Victoria settlement ruins at Port Essington. Sir Thomas Mitchell, with Kennedy second-in-command, was originally obsessed with discovering an overland route to Port Essington until he found that Leichhardt had beaten him to it.

Encouraged by the good country of the Maranoa region, Mitchell crossed more rivers, following the Belyando almost to its junction with the Suttor before returning to the Warrego. He then turned west and, about ten months after leaving Sydney, arrived at a river flowing to the north-west—*the realisation of my long-cherished hopes,* Mitchell recorded. Always on the lookout for imperial brownie points, he named this river the 'Victoria', after the Queen of England.

Kennedy took his duties very seriously on this expedition, even though he was forced to wait behind at a depot on the Maranoa River while Mitchell and a few men forged ahead. Kennedy and the rest of the team were to look after the remaining stores and animals, and plant and nurture a vegetable garden. This work was a far cry from the exploration that had originally enticed him to join Mitchell's party, but not being a man to waste time, Kennedy taught himself the finer points of celestial navigation. When Mitchell returned over four months later, he noted *that the whole establishment evinced the good effects of order and discipline.*

Next year, 1847, Kennedy volunteered his services to lead an expedition that would follow Mitchell's 'Victoria' river. Rather than flowing northwards to the Gulf of Carpentaria, however, Kennedy discovered that the 'Victoria' turned south-west to join another river, which he named the Thomson. In fact Kennedy learned that the 'Victoria' was known to Aboriginal people as the Barcoo, and he traced it to the upper reaches of Cooper Creek. Although he didn't return with the news Mitchell had hoped for, Kennedy had discovered 'channel country', one of Australia's most interesting drainage systems, and more grazing land. He had also proved that he was an admirable expedition leader, equal to the hardships and challenges of outback exploration.

In 1848 the New South Wales Government, no doubt encouraged by Leichhardt's recent success, appointed Kennedy to lead a second expedition. It was an ambitious proposal. The idea was to land a party of men with supplies and equipment on the beach at Rockingham Bay, on the north-east coast of Australia. From there they would explore the coastal country all the way up to the tip of Cape York. After resupplying from a vessel that would be waiting at nearby Port Albany, the expedition would head over to the western side of the Cape and explore south to the bottom of the Gulf of Carpentaria. They would then investigate the Gulf country, eventually linking up with one of Mitchell's previously discovered rivers to find their way back to Sydney. It wasn't just a gigantic undertaking—it was mission impossible.

Strangely, the planning of the journey was not left to its leader. The boss, Mitchell, had suggested that Kennedy travel overland to the Gulf of Carpentaria and from there to Cape York. But with Mitchell on leave in Britain, a number of his colleagues got together to nut out a new plan. No less than the Governor of New South Wales, the Colonial Secretary and the marine surveyors Captain Phillip Parker King and Captain

Owen Stanley were involved. In other words, the expedition was designed by a committee. As Stanley was about to start a lengthy survey of the north-eastern waters of Australia on board HMS *Rattlesnake*, he thought it would be a good idea to have Kennedy's expedition working in tangent along the coast. The trouble was, none of these men had any appreciation or understanding of the environment of Cape York Peninsula, or of the geographical enormity of the proposal. Sadly, their plan was based on naivety, and from the very beginning its aim was unachievable.

We don't know what Kennedy thought of the revised game plan, but with his ingrained sense of duty he certainly did not question those in authority. As his journey was predicted to take about 18 months, he was unable to stick to his original idea of travelling lightly. Instead, based on past experiences, he figured he would need 28 horses and three carts to manage the provisions and equipment, and that 100 sheep would be required to feed him and the dozen men selected to accompany the expedition. Little did he know that the gear that had worked in the back blocks of western New South Wales just wasn't suited to the Cape York landscape. Part of the problem was the poor intelligence on which he based his decisions.

Kennedy's selection of expedition members was fairly straightforward, as six of the men had accompanied him previously. These were Mr C Niblett (storekeeper), John Douglas (Kennedy's servant), Mr T Wall (naturalist/ collector), Edward Taylor, James Luff and William Costigan (carters). To this group he added the botanist, Mr William Carron; a friend's servant, Mr Thomas Mitchell; and three convicts: William Goddard, Dennis Dunn and Mr Edward Carpenter. The idea was that if the convicts behaved themselves they'd be free men at the end of the expedition. Goddard, Mitchell, Douglas and Dunn were signed on as labourers, and Carpenter as shepherd for the one hundred sheep. The last minute addition to the team was an Aboriginal guide, Jacky, who came from the Hunter River valley, around Singleton way.

Not long before his scheduled departure for the Cape, Kennedy attended a fancy ball at Government House. He was 29 years old and apparently his good looks and social graces really impressed a certain Colonel Mundy who had recently arrived in Sydney. Mundy wanted to know all about Kennedy, and soon learned of the proposed expedition. *He is a fine fellow*, the informant added, *he will either accomplish his object,*

Botanist William Carron was one of the three men who survived Kennedy's Cape York expedition. Without access to Carron's diary, the fate of Kennedy and nine others would have remained a complete mystery. This shot was taken many years after the expedition.

or leave his bones in the bush. A prophetic statement, as it turned out.

On 29 April 1848, Edmund Kennedy and his men sailed out of Sydney Harbour in the barque *Tam O'Shanter*. In company with the survey ship HMS *Rattlesnake*, the journey to Rockingham Bay took about three weeks, which gave Kennedy plenty of time to sort out his thoughts and catch up on some writing. At an earlier date, his

On 29 April 1848 Edmund Kennedy and his men sailed out of Sydney Harbour in this barque the Tam O'Shanter. *Their journey to Rockingham Bay on Queensland's north coast took about three weeks.*

Jacky of Singleton (centre, front), part of Kennedy's team, was one of the great survivors of Australian exploration.

father had asked him in a letter about his views on Australian Aborigines. In light of events to come, it's interesting to read the following extract of the letter he wrote home:

> *I have paid much attention wherever I have been to their general habits, tastes, and dispositions and I feel convinced that nothing can be done towards civilising the adults. The children might be made anything of by removing them to Van Dieman's Land—or other unconnected land—but whether that would be a justifiable interference or not on the part of the Government I do not pretend to say.*
>
> *I do not think that they are all physically inferior to the white man although no doubt the generality at present are; but might not the second or third generation improve by cultivation? Towards reconciling the natives to our occupation of their land much might be*

done by distributing amongst them Tomahawks and Blankets. An English Tomahawk would be a fortune to a native for it would provide him with food at one tenth the labor he had before; it is a hard days work to cut an opossum out of a tree with their stone Tomahawks, but with an Iron instrument they might accomplish the same in an hour.

The thousands of Pounds that have been spent by the Government in feeding the natives in idleness has proved a perfect failure because it interfered too materially with their former habits. The Australian savage though naturally indolent is of necessity constantly employed from daylight till dark in looking for food and although the labor is but light his mind is occupied but when a number of them are brought together at a Protector's Station and fed in idleness, the time hangs heavily, they are not so well in bodily health and become miserable.

The Roman Catholic Bishop sent for me the day before I left Sydney and requested me to bear in mind while on my Expedition the intention of the R[oman] Cath[olic] Body to form Missionary establishments along the coast so as the better to be able to point out the most suitable points on my return. I feel sure however that the native adults are too far behind in the scale of civilisation to derive any benefit from religious instruction and that it would be equally vain to expect so much from the children when left within the influence of their parents. The New Zealander and South Sea Islanders are a far superior Race of people and therefore it does not at all follow that because the Missionaries have been partially successful with them they should be so here.

I would suspect that starting his journey with these thoughts rattling through his brain was probably not the best way to go. But worse was to come. Captain Phillip Parker King, who had helped change Mitchell's original plan for the expedition, had surveyed parts of the Cape York coastline some 30 years previously. He and Stanley had suggested Rockingham Bay as the best place to start the expedition. King's chart described the country behind the Bay as 'low land apparently occupied by lagoons' and showed a gap in the line of hills. To the north, the Bellenden Ker Range was marked on the chart as 'fine wooded country' and 'low wooded vallies verdant in appearance'. Now it happens that the rugged Bellenden Ker Range contains Queensland's highest peak, Mount Bartle Frere, which rises to over 1600 metres. It would seem that King, no doubt a brilliant marine surveyor, relied more on his imagination than the facts when it came to describing the land.

For a few days after their arrival at Rockingham Bay, Kennedy and some of the crew searched for an appropriate place to unload the expedition members, stores and equipment, which included four dogs as well as the horses and sheep, one ton of flour,

600 lbs of sugar and 90 lbs of tea. There were also plenty of goods and chattles such as tents, harnesses, hobbles, tether ropes, guns, ammunition, boxes and paper for preserving specimens and even a canvas sheepfold for heaven's sake!

What Kennedy saw during these recces must have filled him with horror. Back on board the ship, he confided in a letter to a friend:

I have visited the Bay at three different points, and confess a viler looking country never looked me in the face before. Ranges of 4800 feet (at the highest) encircle the Bay. They are very abrupt and densely wooded . . . I must get inland as soon as possible, as the Coast Range will not permit of travelling with Horse carts.

Finally they decided on a site close to Tam O'Shanter Point, at the northern end of Rockingham Bay. Just getting all the gear ashore presented a major challenge, and in fact one of the horses drowned in the process. After two days, the job was done and Camp I had been established in open scrub near a freshwater creek, a few hundred

At ten o'clock A.M., slings having been prepared, we commenced hoisting the horses out of the hold, and lowering them into the water alongside a boat, to the stern of which the head of each horse was secured, as it was pulled ashore, *according to the narrative of William Carron, botanist on Kennedy's Cape York expedition.*

metres inland from the beach. Each of Kennedy's men was issued some clothes, blankets, guns and ammunition; weekly rations for the 13 men were calculated at 100 lbs of flour, 26 lbs of sugar and three and a half lbs of tea. One sheep would be killed every second day.

Ironically, Kennedy's 'vile country' is now a part of the Wet Tropics World Heritage area, valued for its magnificent landscape of mountain ranges, waterfalls, fast flowing rivers and tropical rainforests. It's also my backyard, and one of my favourite parts of Australia. These days, heading up the Cape is still one of Australia's great four-wheel drive adventures. It takes about 10 to 12 days to travel up and back, allowing for a few side-trips along the way. Needless to say, the more time you have, the more you'll see.

But 150 years ago, without roads, maps and four-wheel drive vehicles, it was a totally different story and Kennedy wasn't too impressed. From his first camp, a small party went to look for a way inland. They reached the top of the first line of ridges behind the coast only to find mangrove and tea-tree swamps, thick rainforest and more ridge lines. All up it took a week of recces to discover that there was no way west.

By 2 June, Kennedy knew his only hope of finding a way inland was to start by heading south. The ships' crews arrived in boats to help them across the Hull River, the northernmost of the six waterways that empty into Rockingham Bay. Kennedy was still optimistic, at least outwardly, and no doubt this helped to inspire confidence in his men. He earned their respect through his example of hard work and by his consideration for their needs.

The sandy beach and intermittent rain made hard going for the carts, and once they got to the Hull it took till 10 pm to ferry all the gear across the river. The ships were due to leave next day, and then Kennedy and his men would be on their own, heading south instead of north. They would have made a pretty circus for the local Aborigines who watched them pass: Kennedy and Jacky riding out front, then the three carts each drawn by three horses, followed by the remaining horses in groups of three. The sheep came next, tailed by Carpenter and the four dogs. Carron was at the end of the procession. The other men travelled with the horses.

They'd almost reached the southern end of Rockingham Bay when a track leading inland to the south-west was discovered. By this time two men were sick with 'ague', a fever of some sort. After three weeks they were about 18 miles from their landing point and still heading in the wrong direction. Just imagine how depressing that would be. You're into a brand new expedition, but after three whole weeks you're still going the wrong way. It was an impossible situation for Kennedy; while that country is awfully nice to look at, it's not much fun to move through, which was exactly Kennedy's problem. More recces showed that steep mountain ranges barred the way inland; to head north they'd have to follow the eastern slopes of these ranges and try to stay above the boggy swamps of the coastal plains.

This was a very wearing business, physically as well as psychologically. The men would have been well aware of the distance they were adding to their journey. Nagging at the backs of their minds would have been the thought that even when they reached the Cape, they still had a long, long way to go. I'm sure it would have helped them enormously if they'd known they could finish the expedition at the tip of the Cape, but that wasn't the case.

To add to the difficulties, relations with the local Aborigines soured. It seems that unbeknown to Kennedy, some of his men had been carrying on with the local women—not a good policy. In response to the Aborigines' threats, the expeditioners opened fire and killed at least one of the Aboriginal people. Now that incident brings out an interesting point, because Kennedy and his men then adopted a sort of 'them and us' mentality, a bit like a siege or fortress attitude, which was to work against them in the long run.

On 6 July the whole expedition moved on. Its progress was painfully slow, what with sick men, and long grass hiding the uneven ground, rocks and fallen logs. There were plenty more watercourses with steep banks, mostly bordered by thick patches of trees. And, of course, the rainforests with their tangled growth of plants presented the biggest problem, especially as the men had to cut a track wide enough for the carts. *Calamus*, commonly known as 'lawyer' or 'wait-a-while' vine, posed the greatest challenge, as Carron described in his journal:

> *It forms a dense thicket, into which it is impossible to penetrate without first cutting it away, and a person once entangled in its long tendrils has much difficulty in extricating himself, as they lay hold of everything they touch.*

The aim of Kennedy's 1848 expedition was to explore the coastal country from Rockingham Bay to the tip of Cape York, shown here. After resupplying from a ship waiting off Albany Island, they planned to travel to the western side of the Cape and explore south to the bottom of the Gulf of Carpentaria. They would then investigate the Gulf country, eventually making their way back to Sydney. Of the original party of 13 men, only Jacky, the Aboriginal guide from Singleton, made it to the tip of the Cape.

Of all the rainforest plants, Calamus sp – commonly known as 'lawyer vine' posed the greatest challenge for Kennedy and his party, as botanist Carron described: a person once entangled in its long tendrils has much difficulty in extricating himself, as they lay hold of everything they touch.

Calamus gets the name of 'lawyer vine' because it's a bit like lawyers—once you get caught up with them it's almost impossible to get away. But the rainforest country is full of the stuff. What Kennedy was trying to do was to get his expedition on top of the Atherton Tableland. I shudder whenever I think of the task he was hoping to accomplish.

Kennedy, however, was an eternal optimist and always hoped conditions would improve. But they didn't, and on 14 July he finally decided to abandon the carts. Of course that also meant leaving behind everything that was heavy or awkward to carry, including Carron's specimen box. Funny thing, that. Every time those exploring parties had a cartage problem, the first thing to be dumped was the botanists' specimens. It happened time and time again: Kennedy, Leichhardt and Stuart all did it at some stage. For Kennedy's team it meant that from then on nobody could ride, as all of the horses were needed to carry the gear.

One of the things that really frustrates me about this story is the waste of effort during the first month of the expedition. That's when the men were at their fittest and most enthusiastic, with high energy levels—all of that momentum was wasted. Had they landed further to the south, say around the Townsville area, they could have walked straight inland and bypassed the rainforest country that gave them so much trouble.

Well, after negotiating a way out of the Tully gorge up a steep mountain spur, the party reached a point just above Tully Falls. Jacky was proving to be by far the best team member. He was a cheerful, hard worker whose bush skills were unrivalled. From the upper reaches of the Tully River, the country opened up as they headed out towards Mount Garnet. But creeks, stony ridges, gullies and rough, irregular ground still challenged them. Then to Kennedy's great disappointment he learned that his trusted storekeeper had been stealing food. You can't really blame him—they simply weren't getting enough to eat. Mind you, I've never understood why you'd put a man called Nibblett in charge of the tucker.

The loss of food meant a drastic cut in rations for the whole party and Carron noted on 5 August, *We now made up our minds for the first time, to make our horses, when too weak to travel, available for food.* What a quaint way of putting it—'available

Carron recorded that Mr Kennedy's tent was 8 feet long, by 6 feet, and 8 feet high; and in it were placed a compact table, constructed with joints so as to fold up, a light, lamp, stool, his books and instruments.

*Heathlands, lakes and sand
dunes characterise coastal
country at Shelburne Bay, seen
here after heavy rain.*

*Cooper Creek in a good year
teems with catfish, yellowbelly,
bream, freshwater crayfish and
mussels. For thousands of years
the local Aboriginal people
thrived on these and other food
resources. It has never ceased to
amaze me that during the time
they spent here, Burke and Wills
made no real attempt to do
likewise.*

Cape York's landscape is as rugged as it is spectacular. Dozens of waterfalls like this one, north of Jacky's Pudding Pan Hill, spring to life following the annual wet season. Some of these waterfalls have only recently been put on the map.

for food'. 'Righto, Neddy, you are now available for food.' Mind you, they'd already lost a fair number of animals due to the difficult conditions of travel and the scarcity of feed.

Another thing about this expedition that really strikes me is how little use the men made of the natural resources that surrounded them. The large numbers of healthy-looking Aborigines living on the Cape were proof enough that bush tucker existed in the area. I can understand them not wanting to have a go at the local plant food—that's fair enough—but they didn't even really try to catch fish until circumstances further north at Weymouth Bay forced them to have a go. Of course the Cape York coastline is abundant with food, including the famous Queensland mud crab. They could even have tried the dreaded mangrove worm, but somehow I think that may have been a bit much for them. Anyway, it seems that the expeditioners attempted to eat only those things that they were most familiar with: the sheep and even the horses. Only on a couple of occasions did they try the local kangaroo or wallabies. It's an age-old hangup, really.

At the end of the last century, an observer of the Aboriginal people living on the Cape wrote:

The quantity and variety of fruits, nuts and roots in this vast garden of nature, and the numerous streams teeming with fish with which this country is so lavishly endowed, and shell-fish on the coast, provides them with an easily acquired and abundant living.

This idyllic description is a bit exaggerated, of course, but still contrasts with the expedition's daily grind of long days and hard work. The men would take turns to keep watch at night, so no one ever had an uninterrupted sleep. Before dawn the man on watch would call Carron to supervise the cook's preparation of breakfast—hot tea, damper and meat. Now, a diet like that leaves a lot to be desired. Most of the cooking was done the night before; by daybreak it was divided into 13 portions. They had to start early because it was impossible to travel through the heat of late mornings and early afternoons.

Straight after breakfast the men would decamp, round up the sheep, saddle the horses, load up and set off. Only men who were really sick or weak were permitted to ride. By mid-morning they'd be looking for shade and water to stop and rest. Very occasionally they tried hunting or fishing, but without much luck. When the worst of the day's heat was over they'd march till evening, looking for a camping place with water and feed for animals. There was no food for lunch; dinner was the same as breakfast: damper, mutton and tea. It was hard work setting up camp and attending to all the duties.

It's no surprise that the men were famished and exhausted. Their energy levels must have been very low, and I would have to blame a lot of that on their inadequate diet. During the entire expedition, a kangaroo, a few wallabies, emus, ducks and other birds were shot on very rare occasions; in addition a couple of fish, and some pandanus, figs, palm seeds, portulaca and nondas made an irregular and very minor supplement to their boring diet.

The nonda, a sort of bush plum, had been described by Ludwig Leichhardt, and Carron was quick to identify it: *an oblong yellow fruit, having a rough stone inside; the part covering the stone has, when ripe, a mealy appearance, and very good flavour.*

Men and animals suffered from the shortage of food. They couldn't afford to waste

*Black-lipped oysters (*Saccostrea echinata*) are just like rock oysters except that they're a bit 'mouth puckering' due to the abundance of iodine I believe.*

*Nonda plums (*Parinaria nonda*) sustained Jacky during his ten day dash from the site of Kennedy's death to the tip of Cape York and rescue. These plums are only found on Cape York Peninsula and in the Gulf country. Leichhardt was the first white person to note their presence.*

anything; wool from the sheep was used to stuff saddles, offal from horses cooked and eaten, blood used to make 'blood pudding'. I'm sure that giving it a fancy name helped the eating considerably. But the lack of proper nourishment led to a rapid decline in health and morale. Because the men had no knowledge of the local bush tucker they soon discovered that overeating or lack of food preparation could result in serious health problems. But I guess back in those days, the attitude towards food was that as long as the stomach felt as though it had something in it, what more could you want?

You see, by now Kennedy had really painted himself into a corner. With resupply points pegged at fixed times in fixed places and so much time wasted just trying to find a way inland, he really had to move fast to try to catch up. He would have been far better off if he'd had time to stop and rest along the way, regroup and then press on. Instead he was tied to commitments and had to keep going.

On 16 September the expedition reached the Mitchell River, almost one-third of the way to Port Albany. But every time conditions improved something terrible would happen. The men were starving and always trying to steal food, which was guarded jealously. North of the Mitchell the behaviour of the Aborigines was totally unpredictable and relations between them and the expeditioners grew hostile, as Carron recorded:

> *Twelve or fourteen natives made their appearance at the camp this evening, from the same direction as on the previous day. Each one was armed with a large bundle of spears, and with boomerangs. Their bodies were painted with a yellowish earth, which, with their warlike gestures, made them look very ferocious.*

These Aboriginal people set fire to the grass around the camp site and then moved in close enough to throw spears at the intruders. Kennedy's men opened fire, and the attackers fled. Psychologically the whole team was now on a defensive footing. The siege mentality was really coming into action.

Despite a shortage of fresh water, they were now making better progress—about 12 miles a day—and heading almost due north. But the sandy ridges and marshy flats made hard going for the horses and sheep, and the men's spirits were failing. By the end of September they were nearing Princess Charlotte Bay, almost two months late for their scheduled rendezvous with HMS *Bramble*.

Once again, the marine surveyors had blown it. Judging by their charts, it was a

Passing outside of the Palm Islands, and rounding Cape Sandwich, we entered Rockingham Bay, and anchored on the N.W. side of Goold Island, where we found the *Tam O'Shanter* . . . The natives, a small party of whom were here, have had frequent intercourse with Europeans, and indeed the sight alongside the ship of eight canoes, four of which carried two unarmed men, and the others one each, would of itself, to most people, have been a convincing proof of a friendly disposition. *This descriptive passage was recorded by John MacGillivray in* Narrative of the Voyage of HMS Rattlesnake, during the Years 1846–1850.

The next morning, May 30th, Mr Kennedy and three others of the party rode out to examine the surrounding country, and to determine in what direction the expedition should start. *Botanist William Carron recorded in his journal the expedition's day-to-day activities as well as detailed descriptions of Cape York's plants.*

perfect rendezvous point, but in reality the bay is very shallow near the shore: a vast expanse of estuaries, mudflats, swamps and mangroves. By mid-October, having got within ten miles of the Bay but unable to proceed any further, Kennedy and his men turned northwest. By then the expedition was way overdue, and in any case Kennedy figured that the *Bramble* would have moved on.

By this time there was so little sugar left it had to be kept for emergencies. The flour supply was down to 200 pounds, but still no serious attempt was made to live off the land. As they moved further north, the different groups of Aborigines they encountered alternated between bringing food and fresh water into camp and seriously threatening the men. It was a mixed bag in many ways; sometimes the local Aborigines took no notice of the expedition, and at other times quite the opposite reaction emerged.

The lowland rainforest and stony ridges around Lockhart River really took its toll on the expeditioners, and on 11 November the wilting party set up Camp 80 near Weymouth Bay. With most of his men now quite ill, and with an acute shortage of supplies and time, Kennedy decided to leave eight men at this camp under supervision of the botanist, Carron. Of the eight, six men would die there—one of the biggest tragedies in the history of Australian exploration. It's still possible to identify the site, thanks to the description given by Carron in his journal:

We crossed the creek where it turned eastward, on a kind of bank, which intercepted its course, up to which, from the east, the tide came sometimes, so that on that side [of] the creek the water was brackish, but very good water was obtainable on the other side [of] the bank.

The site of Camp 80 is a really remote place, and even these days there are no roads in there. If you want to see it, you've got to go on foot or by helicopter. The spot is set back from the coastline a few miles and is fed by a small saltwater creek which, as Carron described, turns into freshwater where a sandbar crosses it. On the southern side of the creek a hill takes off and it was on the hill's lower slopes that Kennedy set up his Weymouth Bay camp.

It's quite a pretty place, with the vegetation closing in around the winding creek and backing on to the more open woodland to the south. When you walk down to the creek, it's quite easy to identify the exact patch of ground that Kennedy used to get across. In many ways it's not too hard to visualise the scene there even today, and I'm sure the cool water of that creek was at least some relief to the dying men. Half the attraction for me was the fact that virtually no white person had been back there on the ground since the 1840s. It was really an amazing feeling.

On 13 November, with 200 kilometres of unknown country between them and the tip of the Cape, Kennedy, Jacky, Costigan, Dunn and Luff prepared to leave. Kennedy left written instructions for Carron. He was to keep a look-out for the rescue ship from higher ground, raising a flag on a makeshift pole and signalling whether or not the Aborigines were friendly. In the meantime, he was to log thermometer readings and maintain discipline in camp. Kennedy also suggested that Carron try to make his meagre rations last for six weeks, as he had no idea at the time just how long it would take to reach the ship and return for his men.

In north Queensland's tropical rainforests, like this one inland from Mission Beach, waterfall spray promotes the growth of water-loving plants such as mosses and ferns.

I packed up all the dried meat we had left (75 lbs) and 18 lbs of flour for Mr Kennedy to take with him, and about one pound of tea was divided between the two parties. These, with their firearms, and a few necessaries of a light description, were all the party took with them.

From that remote, isolated campsite, judging from Carron's journal entry, it must have been an awful feeling to wave goodbye to the departing men:

Wearied out by long endurance of trials that would have tried the courage and shaken the fortitude of the strongest, a sort of sluggish indifference prevailed, that prevented the development of those active energies which were so necessary to support us in our critical position.

The men who stayed at that camp developed the siege mentality towards the local Aborigines I described earlier. They did not trust them at all. They jumped at everything that moved, and stayed awake for half the night. This frame of mind is really psychologically defeating, particularly when you're already weak and sick. You've got little energy as a result of a poor diet, but then on top of that you lie awake all night, frightened by every noise the bush makes, and suddenly you find yourself in a really hopeless situation that continues day after day, night after night.

Kennedy and his party found much flatter country north of the Pascoe River, but

The tragic story of the explorer,
Edmund Besley Court Kennedy,
has been with me ever since, as
a young schoolboy, I saw a
picture like this in my Social
Studies text book.

the heat was absolutely horrendous. On 18 November they used the last of their flour, and on the following day, according to Jacky,

> *we stopped at a little creek and it came on raining, and Costigan shot himself; in putting his saddle under the tarpaulin, a string caught the trigger and the ball went in under the right arm and came out at his back under the shoulder.*

They pushed on for a bit, but with Costigan still in pain and Luff quite sick, Kennedy was forced to leave them under Dunn's care at Camp 84. This place means a lot to me. In 1971, while I was still in the Army, I put together an expedition to go and find this campsite. To my knowledge no one had been there since 1848, and I was keen to do so. You see, the three men who'd been left there—Costigan, Dunn and Luff—vanished. They were never seen or heard of again.

I decided to take leave from the army with three of my mates and head for Cape York Peninsula in search of Camp 84. Before we left I went to visit the late Edgar Beale, who was a real authority on Kennedy. There's an old military saying that the Army had really drummed into us: 'Prior preparation beats poor performance'. With his two excellent books, *Kennedy of Cape York* and *Kennedy Workbook*, Beale steered me in the right direction. That was the only time I spent with Edgar Beale, but I'll never forget it. On my bookshelf at home is a copy of *Kennedy of Cape York*, which Beale presented to me, writing in the front cover: *For Les Hiddins, with the compliments and best wishes of one Kennedy enthusiast for another—author to on-the-spot investigator.*

Beale's contribution to my Kennedy research was of great significance, and I'm sure that without his guidance our search for Camp 84 would have had a very different result. Our small party managed to find the creek line along which the camp had been established 127 years previously. It was a tough job and really gave us a feeling for what Kennedy and his men had experienced.

Of the original team of 13, with a few hundred kilometres to go, only Jacky and Kennedy were fit enough to continue. They had to get to the resupply ship and return for the men as quickly as possible. Before leaving Camp 84, Kennedy sent Jacky to the top of a nearby hill to get a fix on some landmarks so they'd know where to come back to for the men. It was a weird feeling for me to climb that same hill, 13 kilometres

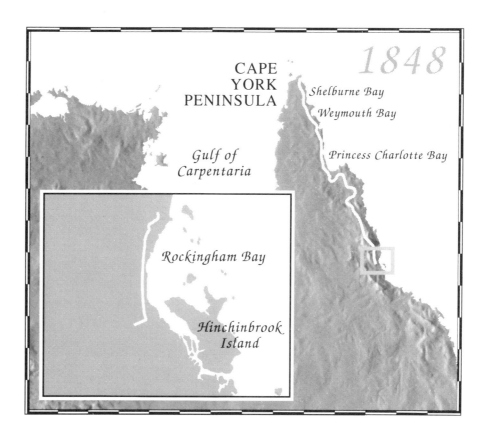

inland from Shelburne Bay, over 120 years later. I could quite well imagine that no one had been to the top since that day so long ago, when Jacky stood there looking out to sea. Touching history like that for the first time is addictive, and like no other feeling that I can think of.

Over the years there's been a bit of confusion about the name of this hill. At the time Jacky called it Pudding Pan Hill, but for me it will always be Jacky's Pudding Pan Hill.

Kennedy and Jacky left Camp 84 with some dried horse meat and about half a dozen horses in a desperate bid to reach the ship. The two men were now almost totally dependent·on each other. They struggled over ridges and creeks, through gullies and swamps. Every so often they'd lose another horse along the way. Heavy rain began to fall, as the wet season was closing in fast, and all around, according to Jacky:

there were plenty of blacks here, but we did not see them, but plenty of fresh tracks, and
camps, and smoke.

Finally they reached the mouth of the Escape River, right up near the tip of Cape

York. To their great relief, they could just see in the distance a ship anchored off nearby Albany Island. But before they could reach the shore to signal the ship they first had to get around the Escape River. That's easier said than done. The Escape River is a few hundred metres wide at its mouth where the two men struck it, and it gets even wider a little further upstream. To find a crossing they had to duck and dive in and out of the thick scrub that lines the bank to check on the width of the river. Even getting close to the bank is a battle—it's wetland country bordered by thick scrub of rainforest and mangroves, and in places it's a sort of strange mixture of the two.

The river narrows suddenly about 15 kilometres from its mouth. That's where Jacky tried to get Kennedy to cross, but at the time Kennedy was just about done in and wanted to continue on horseback. I somehow suspect that Kennedy simply didn't have the energy or the strength left to try to swim. Little did the two men know, but the local Aboriginal people were about to turn hostile. For days they'd been tracking

On his way to the tip of Cape York, Kennedy set up his Camp 84 13 kilometres inland from Shelburne Bay, a magnificent area of white sand dunes, lakes, heath and rainforest. Three men remained in this camp: one had accidentally shot himself, another was very ill and the third was pretty weak. None of them was ever seen again.

I call this 185 metre, flat-topped hill, 'Jacky's Pudding Pan Hill'. Kennedy sent Jacky up to the summit to get a fix on some landmarks so he'd recognise the place when they returned with the rescue ship to pick up the men left behind at Camp 84.

Kennedy and Jacky, and Jacky was really concerned. He advised Kennedy to keep looking behind him and also tried to talk him into abandoning the horses, so that they could move more stealthily, but Kennedy was too weak and wouldn't hear of it. In his mind, Kennedy was convinced that these Aborigines were friendly.

Then suddenly, according to Jacky,

a good many black fellows came behind in the scrub, and threw plenty of spears, and hit Mr Kennedy in the back first . . . I pulled out the spear at once from Mr Kennedy's back, and cut out the jag with Mr Kennedy's knife; then Mr Kennedy got his gun and snapped, but the gun would not go off. The blacks sneaked all along by the trees, and speared Mr Kennedy again in the right leg, above the knee a little, and I got speared over the eye, and the blacks were now throwing their spears always, never giving over, and shortly again speared Mr Kennedy in the right side; there were large jags to the spears, and I cut them out and put them into my pocket.

Before long, Kennedy died in the arms of his faithful friend. Jacky buried him in a shallow grave and waited till dark to leave. It's forlorn country around there. The open plains, swamps and stunted tea-trees give it an eerie atmosphere, or at least that's the way it always appears to me—but then again I'm well acquainted with the past goings on there. Every time I think of that particular patch of Cape York, I think of drizzly rain, because that's the way it's been most times I've been there, and that's the way it was for Kennedy and Jacky.

It was now entirely up to Jacky to reach the ship and try to rescue the other men. During this time he had to survive as best he could. You've got to remember that this wasn't Jacky's country. He was a long way from his own country down in the Hunter Valley, and Cape York was every bit as foreign to him as it was to the rest of the crew. In the 10 days it took him to reach the beach near Somerset, he was forced to wade up to his neck in the crocodile infested Escape River, and to pick up whatever food came within easy reach—pandanus fruit and the good old nonda plum.

Over the years I've thought a lot about how close Kennedy came to reaching his destination. The trouble was, once the original party had been watered down to two men it was much easier for the Aborigines to put in an attack. If only they hadn't wasted all that time at the beginning of the journey, the whole group could have stayed together and made it to the tip of Cape York.

But it wasn't to be. On the morning of 23 December, an exhausted Jacky broke through to the beach, and from the tip of Cape York he signalled the waiting *Ariel*. Of the original party of 13 men, only Goddard, Carron and Jacky survived, and of these three, only Jacky managed to make the journey from Rockingham Bay to the tip of the Cape. On his return to Sydney, Jacky became a national hero. To my mind he remains one of the great figures in Australian exploration.

And, you know, if Jacky hadn't made it to the ship we'd have no information about this expedition at all, because no one else knew where the rest of the men were. Without access to Carron's diary, the fate of Kennedy and his team would have been a complete mystery, just like the disappearance of Ludwig Leichhardt. It's that simple. These days, from a historical point of view, we Australians owe Jacky from Singleton an awful lot.

At Cooper Creek, expedition
leader Robert O'Hara Burke
split his team for the second time
since leaving Melbourne. Four
men would stay and build a
stockade while the others would
set off to break through to the
Gulf.

CHAPTER FOUR

BURKE AND WILLS

THE FIRST TIME I can remember travelling through 'Burke and Wills' country was when I was a youngster up in the Gulf of Carpentaria. Normanton, Croydon, Burketown and Karumba were the local communities. I was only very young then, but I distinctly remember associating the name of Burketown with the two explorers who had travelled from somewhere down south up to the Gulf, then back to a place called Cooper Creek. Being a North Queensland kid, this southern detail didn't concern me too much in those days, but I figured they'd had a pretty hard time of it. Over the years my appreciation of the Burke and Wills venture grew and grew, particularly after I visited their  old campsite on the banks of the Bynoe River outside Burketown and learned about the various routes the search parties took while trying to find the missing explorers.

I'd always known a fair bit about the northern end of their expedition: in February 1861, Burke, Wills, King and Gray had struggled up towards the Gulf with a horse and a few camels. They'd almost reached the sea, but short of time and tucker, they'd turned around and headed back south. Of the four men, only King survived to tell the tale. I also knew that the expedition was Victoria's only real attempt at exploring the vast continent of Australia, and that it had started in Melbourne with a cast of thousands and a lavish array of food and equipment. The fact that it ended up being one of the greatest debacles in Australia's exploration history had left me wondering what went wrong. I think it's worth going back to the Melbourne end of the expedition to have a look.

In 1851 the small colony of Victoria separated itself from New South Wales. During the next few years, following discoveries of huge gold deposits at Ballarat and Bendigo, Victoria's population grew in leaps and bounds. Before long, Australia's youngest colony had become the wealthiest and most heavily populated.

From the earliest days of separation, the Victorians had been keen to prove their worth to the neighbouring colonies of South Australia and New South Wales. The best way of doing this, according to some of the more influential members of society, would be through exploration. With Victoria's boundaries fixed and its own territory pretty well explored, you've got to wonder what the Victorians had to gain by this—apart from praise.

On 19 August 1858, an article in the Melbourne *Argus* newspaper reported, *We are authorised to state that a gentleman of Melbourne proposes to give the sum of £1000 towards the promotion of a judicious scheme of Australian exploration.* But there were strings attached: the donation would be made only if fellow colonists would contribute an additional £2000. The paper went on to announce that rather than using horses or bullocks, the proposed expedition would use camels. Although the press was very excited by the proposal, it took another year to raise the extra money because there was a lack of public interest.

Nevertheless, the Victorians set their sights high. Rather than poking around just beyond the settled districts, they aimed to find an overland route from Melbourne to the Gulf of Carpentaria: a first continental crossing from south to north. To accomplish this goal, however, it was agreed that a dozen or so men would need to spend a fair bit of time on the job. This in turn would require a substantial amount of money—about another £6000.

To kick things along the Royal Society of Victoria held its first meeting early in 1860. It quickly appointed an Exploration Committee of 17 members, two of whom—grazier Angus McMillan and botanist Ferdinand Mueller—had some Australian explo-

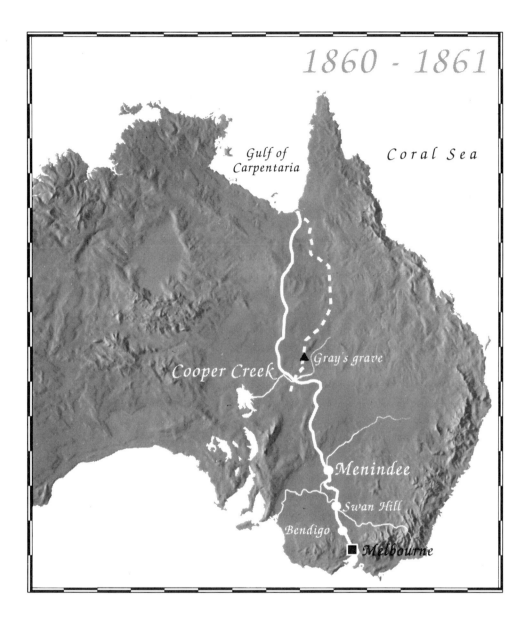

ration experience. Meanwhile the Victorian Government had backed a suggestion to

import camels into the colony. A bloke by the name of George Landells, who'd spent a

lot of time in India, had sailed back there from Melbourne with a load of horses to deliver

to the British Army. Before he left, the Victorian Government had agreed to his suggestion

to buy a few dozen camels that could be used for exploring inland Australia.

With enough money and enthusiasm to support the Victorian Exploring Expedition,

the Committee's next step was to select a leader. The trouble was, no one in Victoria

was suited for the role.

Just how Robert O'Hara Burke came to be chosen is a convoluted story, possibly best summed up by the *Age* newspaper as 'an affair of cliquery'. Apparently even in those days, it wasn't what you knew but whom you knew that counted.

Burke was born in Ireland about 1820. He'd joined the Austrian Army in 1840, and after seven years of undistinguished service was noted as being 'absent without leave'. Burke claimed that this offence occurred partly because of sickness and partly because he'd run up some debts that he was unable to repay. Even today those excuses for going AWOL would be considered pretty weak. He resigned from the army in 1848, and in the following year joined the Irish police force. A few years later, having decided he could make a better living in Australia, Burke secured himself the necessary references and left for Melbourne.

By 1858 Burke was working as Superintendent of Police in the provincial Victorian town of Castlemaine. He'd had no experience of the Australian bush, had no scientific or surveying knowledge, had never drawn a map or even kept a proper journal. He wasn't a particularly good leader, lacked self-control and was well known for his quick temper.

It wasn't up to Burke to choose the Victorian Exploring Expedition's team members; that was a job for the Committee. When George Landells returned to Melbourne with his camels and their exotic-looking drivers in June 1860, practically the whole town turned out to have a look. Landells became an overnight success and was promptly appointed as Burke's second-in-command. He'd spent just a couple of years in Australia and knew even less about the outback than Burke. But at least he was an experienced camel handler and could talk to the Indian camel drivers in their own lingo.

William John Wills, 26 years old, was appointed surveyor and astronomical observer. This was a pretty tall order because it meant that as well as finding the best route for the expedition to follow, he would have to record meteorological and magnetic observations. Wills had left England in 1852 when he was 18, arriving in Australia in January, 1853. He had worked at a few different jobs around Victoria, but by 1855 he'd decided that he wanted to be an explorer, so he joined the district surveyor in Ballarat to learn the finer points of the job. His particular interest was astronomy, and in 1858 he started working at the Observatory in Melbourne.

Captain Charles Sturt named
Cooper Creek in 1845 after
Charles Cooper, then Chief
Justice of South Australia. This
peaceful inland scene was to
become the backdrop for one of
the greatest debacles in the
history of Australian
exploration.

When Burke, Wills, King and Gray set out from their Cooper Creek Depot in a mad dash to beat Stuart to the far north coast, the country they traversed north of the Cooper would have looked a lot like this (without the roadway of course!). Such relatively lush growth of lignum, nardoo and love grasses is only seen when the country has recently flooded.

A few of the more influential Committee members thought that the expedition should be accompanied by scientists and an artist. Burke was opposed to this idea as he felt it would hinder the expedition's progress. Nevertheless the last two officers to be appointed, both Germans, were Hermann Beckler, a doctor whose real interest was natural history (particularly botany); and Ludwig Becker, scientist and artist, and a member of the Royal Society of Victoria.

The job of foreman went to Charles Ferguson, a skilled American horseman. No less than 700 men applied to accompany the expedition, and by mid-July, a dozen or so had been chosen, two of whom—John King and William Brahe—would play a significant part. The team members were aged between 21 and 51, and none had any exploring experience.

Landells had met King in India and offered him a job helping with the camels, mainly because he was able to talk to their drivers. King, an Irishman, had served seven years with the army in India and had bought a discharge. He was recovering from some kind of fever when Landells met him, but quickly accepted the job and went on to join the expedition. Brahe, another German, had arrived in Victoria in 1852. He'd had a few different jobs around the goldfields and was an experienced wagon driver and horseman.

But according to Charles Ferguson, the expedition foreman,

I well remember the remark I made to Mr Burke upon my first visit to the Royal park, where the men were quartered, when he asked me what I thought of them. I told him if I could have my way I would select my men from some of the old experienced bush-men in the prison, rather than start out across the continent with such raw recruits; that I did not believe one-half of them could harness up a team and drive it. And my assertion proved even more than true, for there was not even one man among them that could put together a four-horse team and drive it afterwards.

The game plan for the expedition was to travel from Melbourne through the settled districts to the Darling River. Scientific work would begin in earnest as the expedition moved up to Cooper Creek, where a depot would be established. From the depot the men would begin their exploration of the interior and keep a look out for traces of the missing explorer, Ludwig Leichhardt. They would also attempt to reach the continent's northern shore.

The Committee let it be known that no expense would be spared in outfitting the expedition. Even though experienced explorers had learned that wagons, carts and drays were not suited to travelling through the Australian outback, Burke ordered three large American-style wagons to transport the expedition equipment. As his gear and supplies accumulated—including 80 pairs of boots, a dozen tents, 20 camp beds, four dozen fishing lines, an oak table, 60 gallons of rum (for the camels, would you believe!)—additional wagons had to be hired.

This stone monument in Melbourne's Royal Park marks the departure point for the ill-fated Burke and Wills expedition of 1860–61.

On Monday 20 August, the Victorian Exploring Expedition finally made its grand departure from Melbourne's Royal Park. A brass band and some 10 000 well-wishers cheered the team of 19 men on its way. The quarter-mile long procession of camels, horses and wagons looked more like a circus than an exploring party. Of the 21 tons of supplies and equipment, just 18 000 pounds were food—flour, sugar, meat, tea, coffee and tobacco. Aware of the ravaging effects of scurvy, Burke included tinned vegetables, dried fruit and copious quantities of lime juice; at least in this direction his thinking was correct.

On the outskirts of Melbourne near Moonee Ponds, heavy rain turned the dirt roads to mud and slowed down the procession; some of the overloaded wagons got completely bogged. The rain continued, but as they inched northwards Ferguson recalled:

The caravan caused no little commotion in traversing the settled portion of the country embracing the first few hundred miles. Cattle and horses along the route stampeded from terror at the sight and even at the smell of the camels . . . Men, women and children along the line and from stations and ranches many miles distant came in to see the camels, and in nearly every instance the black natives, to whom the camels were alike a curiosity and a dread, compared them to the emu, for the reason, I suppose, of their long necks . . .

A week's travel took them through the settled districts—green, rolling plains and hills—to the shanty goldmining town of Bendigo on the Campaspe River. As they continued north, the hills gave way to flat plains dotted with swamps. According to Becker,

On you go, miles and miles: a single tree, a belt of timber, appear at the horizon, affected by the mirage. You reach that belt of small trees, a wallaby, a kangaroo-rat disturbs for a moment the monotony and a few steps further on you are again on a green calm ocean.

The camels and horses didn't get along too well, and for that reason they marched in two separate columns, camels on the left and horses on the right. Burke rode between the two.

By 6 September the front end of the party had reached Swan Hill, a small town on the banks of the Murray River. They'd been underway for three weeks; the tail end of the expedition was now three days behind and Burke knew they'd have to get cracking. He decided to call a halt and work out a new plan while waiting for the wagons to catch up. Meanwhile the expedition members who'd made it to Swan Hill were treated to hearty outback hospitality.

Burke now understood that he'd brought far too much gear, so he decided to auction some of it. He'd also received a message from the Committee to say he was

The Burke and Wills expedition passed through the Bendigo goldfields on their way to Cooper Creek from Melbourne. Huge gold deposits had been discovered in the area during the early 1850s.

overspending; it suggested he ditch the hired wagons (a suggestion Burke chose to ignore) and get a move on. He did, however, discharge four of his men and employ another three, including a local Swan Hill bloke, Charlie Gray.

It took several days to ferry animals, stores and equipment across the mighty Murray River, which forms the border between Victoria and New South Wales. By mid-September they'd reached the outpost of Balranald on the Murrumbidgee River, but Burke's problems were far from over. The wagons were still dragging the chain, the hired ones accumulating more expense; the male camels were fighting over the females, and all the camels were fighting with the horses. What's more, the camels tended to wander off whenever they could. Burke ditched another load of equipment and stores, including eight demijohns of lime juice. He also dismissed three more men, one of whom was Ferguson, the foreman. It seems that it wasn't just the camels and horses that weren't getting along with each other.

Burke and a small party of men and animals moved ahead of the wagons through the Mallee country of south-western New South Wales. The dry, flat, sandy terrain posed enormous difficulties for the horses pulling the wagons. Unlike Burke and his men, I find this Mallee country quite interesting in its own way. Mallee, a type of eucalypt, has an unusual way of growing: a number of trunk-like branches of roughly equal size sprout from one large woody lump (or lignotuber, as it's called). The woody lump usually lies underground, but its upper surface is often exposed by erosion. These twisted, hard 'mallee roots' provide excellent, lasting heat to camp fires. Mallee trees can live up to 400 years—which means some of them would have been around the place when Burke and his party went past.

The sandy ground slowed down the wagons so much that Burke was forced to transfer the bulk of their load to the camels. He instructed the men to reduce their personal gear to a maximum of 30 pounds each, adding that from now on the animals would be needed to carry loads and the men would have to *walk, inch for inch, all the way up the Gulf of Carpentaria*. He also ordered Becker and Beckler to abandon their scientific work.

Burke and Landells had never seen eye to eye, and now they started to argue about the camels. Landells considered himself the absolute authority and resented any interference or criticism. But Burke was in command, and he'd soon find a convenient excuse to dismiss Landells.

In early October, Burke's squabbling party reached Menindee, which in those days was known as Laidley Ponds. Menindee, an Aboriginal word meaning 'many waters', is a much more appropriate name, because it describes the country where the Darling River empties itself into a number of swamps and lakes, some of which are permanent. Menindee was a logical departure point for inland Australia; as the country to the north is generally pretty dry, this would have been the last supply of reliable water before Cooper Creek, and an obvious place to set up camp and wait for the rest of the expedition.

With his straggling team still overloaded and plagued by disagreements and worsening financial problems, Burke now learned that John McDouall Stuart, the well known South Australian explorer, was preparing to leave Adelaide in another attempt to cross the continent. From this point onwards Burke saw his expedition as a race against Stuart.

Ten kilometres down the track at Kinchega, an outlying sheep station on the Darling River, some of the stationhands got stuck into the camels' rum. Burke was furious, but what did he really expect? Anyway, he ended up refusing to take the grog any further. Landells decided to quit the whole thing and head back to Melbourne. Beckler also resigned, but agreed to hang around until a replacement arrived.

Ruins of the old Kinchega sheep station are now part of Kinchega national park. Burke and Wills and their party stopped here and added William Wright, bushman and ex-station manager, to their team.

It was now time for a serious reshuffle. Burke promoted Wills to 2IC, put King in charge of the camels and appointed Brahe as the new foreman. William Wright, a bushman and ex-station manager from Kinchega, was added to the team. At Kinchega, the locals echoed the explorer Augustus Gregory's warning to Burke about the hazards of heading north in summer—in particular the searing temperatures and unreliable waterholes. But their advice fell on deaf ears. Instead, Burke decided to split the expedition into two groups, a small, light party would leave for Cooper Creek while the rest remained at the Menindee depot. This rear party would follow on in due course with the heavy stores.

On 19 October the advance party of eight men pushed on across a series of low ridges and dry gibber plains. They took 16 camels, 15 horses and a modest supply of food and stores. Wright, who knew the country ahead, would accompany them for a few days, before returning to take charge of the Menindee depot.

Ironically, now that they were breaking new ground, the scientists (with the exception of Wills) had been left behind. Burke's party passed through Mootwingee, an amazing area whose fossil records tell us all about the inland sea that used to be there. It was also a really important place for the local Aboriginal people who held tribal ceremonies there. They left a record of their day-to-day life in their artwork amongst the rocky outcrops.

Past Mootwingee the expedition headed across the seemingly endless plains, marching from creek to creek. After 320 kilometres they stopped at Torowoto Swamp and Wright turned back, carrying a letter from Burke to the Committee which read in part,

> *Mr Wright returns from here to Menindie. I informed him that I should consider him third officer of the expedition, subject to the approval of the Committee, from the day of our departure from Menindie, and hope that they will confirm the appointment. In the meantime I have instructed him to follow me up with the remainder of the camels to Cooper's Creek . . . If Mr Wright is allowed to follow out the instructions I have given him I am confident that the result will be satisfactory.*

Beyond Torowoto Swamp the dry, rocky country slowed their progress, but there was still water in the creeks and enough feed for the animals. During this part of the journey the men saw very few Aborigines. They pushed on, crossing low ridges and gibber plains and at last, on 11 November, the advance party arrived at Cooper Creek, a series of deep waterholes surrounded by eucalypts, mulga and polygonum grass.

Well, as soon as they made camp, a plague of rats attacked, so they continued on downstream to find a better spot. The rats were *Rattus villosissimus*—the native, long-haired variety. On the northern bank of a magnificent stretch of water full of fish and mussels they established Camp 65—near a big coolabah tree. In spite of the heat (it was about 43 degrees in the shade) the surrounding trees teemed with birdlife.

The Aboriginal people of Cooper Creek welcomed the arrival of the expeditioners, but this welcome was misinterpreted by Wills, who later wrote:

A large tribe of blacks came pestering us to go to their camp and have a dance, which we declined. They were very troublesome and nothing but the threat to shoot will keep them away; they are, however, easily frightened, and, although fine-looking men, decidedly not of a war-like disposition . . . from the little we have seen of them, they appear to be mean-spirited and contemptible in every respect.

Boy, was he in for a shock.

From Camp 65 the men tried in small groups to find a way to the north-west that would link up with the route of explorer Augustus Gregory, but as Burke recorded,

a practicable route cannot be established in that direction, except during the rainy season, or by sinking wells, as the natives have evidently abandoned that part of the country for want of water, which is shown by their having sunk for water in all directions in the bed of the creeks.

By mid-December there was still no sign of Wright, but with enough stores at the Cooper Creek depot Burke wasn't concerned. He decided there was no need to wait, because the rear party would appear any day. The time had finally come to get on with the real adventure—reaching the northern shore of the continent. Once again he decided to split his party. Four men would stay at Cooper Creek and build a stockade while the others would set off to break through to the Gulf, travelling along Eyres Creek. Now just why they felt they had to build a stockade I'm not quite sure,

but the fact that these were the orders tells us a bit about their attitude toward the locals.

Burke promoted Brahe to the rank of officer and put him in charge of the Cooper Creek depot. Burke left no written instructions for Brahe, but he was convinced he could make it to the Gulf of Carpentaria and back again in well under three months. If for some reason he hadn't returned by then, Brahe was to wait as long as his provisions would allow before returning with his men to the Darling.

Burke wrote a note to the Committee reporting that:

the feed upon this creek is good and the horses and camels have greatly improved in condition; but the flies, mosquitoes and rats which abound here render it a very disagreeable summer residence.

Now I can't vouch for the rats and mosquitoes, but I can for the flies. Of course the fly population varies to some extent according to the time of year and the amount of rainfall, but rarely have I encountered the numbers of flies that I did at Cooper

The Menindee pub has had a few facelifts since Robert O'Hara Burke stayed here in 1860. Menindee, an Aboriginal word meaning 'many waters' was a logical departure point for the inland.

Creek. There were millions of them and we became intimate friends during the time I spent there; in fact I still have their names and addresses. I don't envy the men who stayed at the depot one little bit in this regard.

Before leaving, the men killed two horses and jerked the meat, cutting it into strips and drying it in the sun. They then split up the provisions; Burke and his men took 3 hundredweight of flour, 50 pounds of oatmeal, 100 pounds of dried horseflesh, 100 pounds of bacon and salt pork, 30 pounds of biscuit, 50 pounds of rice, 50 pounds of sugar, 12 pounds of tea, 5 pounds of salt and a few tins of vegetables and butter. They also took guns and ammunition for shooting game along the way. On 16 December—mid-summer—they set out for the Gulf against the best advice. They had no doctor, no tents, no maps and no way of communicating with the rest of their team. It would be fair to say that the Victorian Exploring Expedition had now been reduced to a race against John McDouall Stuart.

From Cooper Creek to the Gulf of Carpentaria and back is a journey of 2400 kilometres. The four men (Burke, Wills, King and Gray) started their journey by following Cooper Creek for a few days till they reached Captain Charles Sturt's old track, around the present day town of Innamincka. Then they headed north-west into Channel country where there was plenty of water. They crossed sandy ridges covered with spinifex, (or porcupine grass as it's sometimes called), and on 22 December, they arrived at Sturt's Stony Desert, which Wills described in his journal as *nothing more or less than stony rises that we had before met with, only on a larger scale, and not quite as undulating . . . we thought it far from bad travelling ground.* On the other side they struck the Diamantina River, which fortunately had plenty of water.

Burke and Wills walked in front, taking turns to keep their compass course; Gray followed with the horse and then King with the camels. They quickly established a daily routine, rising at dawn, walking for a couple of hours, stopping for breakfast, then walking till the midday heat forced a stop for lunch. When it got too hot to walk during the day, they'd wait till dark, which was smart thinking. As there was enough water lying around, they looked for campsites that would provide feed for the animals.

The men's daily rations amounted to one pound of damper, three-quarters of a pound of dried horsemeat, one quarter of a pound of salt pork, an eighth of a pound of boiled rice, some tea and sugar. Vitamins were supplied by portulaca or pigweed whenever they could find it. Apart from that, they spared no time for hunting, fishing or gathering bush tucker.

By early January they were well on course, following Eyre's Creek. Nights were cool and there was still no real shortage of water. On 11 January Wills recorded, *The country traversed has the most verdant and cheerful aspect, abundance of feed and water everywhere.*

On 20 January, as they passed just west of the present day town of Cloncurry, the wet season was gathering force. After a month of traversing little more than flat plains, the monotony was broken by the Selwyn Range. Burke elected to travel straight over the top of the Selwyns—I reckon this would have been a taxing route in those conditions. Following the Cloncurry River north, they arrived at its junction with the Flinders towards the end of January, and from there moved on to the little Bynoe River. Heavy rain had made the surrounding flat land a sea of mud where the exhausted camels floundered uselessly. Camels' feet are designed to deal with dry, sandy conditions—which is why you normally find them in the desert.

Queensland's Gulf country is typified by mangroves, mudflats and tidal channels. Here you see the flat Gulf country (which has a gradient of 1:50,000) after the wet season combined with a king tide.

Bulldust!—that's what you stir up when you drive through Gulf country during the dry season. The dust is very fine and it gets into absolutely everything.

In the dry season, the men could have almost walked right down the Bynoe to the shores of the Gulf of Carpentaria. The last 15 kilometres or so sees the Bynoe snaking its way to the Gulf, and of course in that area it weaves through the mudflats and mangrove country that typify the Gulf country. But because of the wet, Burke and Wills were forced to leave the miserable camels with King and Gray at Camp 119 while they set out with the horse to reach the Gulf. This camp-site is well marked today, with a small vehicle track leading in from the main road. It's on the high ground a little to the east of the Bynoe River.

Back in those days, the wetlands, grassy plains and eucalypt scrub at the bottom of the Gulf supported thousands of Aboriginal people, who thrived on the plentiful food supplies—waterbirds, emus, kangaroos and so on. It wasn't too long before Burke and Wills struck a well used footpath that took them to a recently abandoned Aboriginal camp-site. The men scavenged some yams they found lying on the ground and pressed on. Crossing a marsh, Wills recorded that they passed:

> three blacks, who, as is universally their custom, pointed out to us, unasked, the best part down. This assisted us greatly, for the ground we were taking was very boggy. We moved slowly down, about three miles, and then camped for the night.

While I'm not exactly sure of this camp-site location, I have heard stories about another 'B&W' blazed tree beside the Bynoe in this very area. The old stockman who told me about it said he first saw it 40 years ago, while he was working in a mustering camp. I suspect, from the location he described to me, that the carved tree he saw would mark the camp location that Burke and Wills established on the night of 10 February, or perhaps the next day. Anyway, as far as I'm aware, no one has recorded the exact location of this tree, and the task still remains to be done. But if you're thinking of heading out that way, make sure you take your mozzie repellent.

On 11 February, Burke and Wills finally reached their furthest point north. Impenetrable mangrove swamps stopped them from reaching the shores of the Gulf of Carpentaria, so they contented themselves with tasting the salt water that swept over the plain at high tide. According to Burke, *It would be well to say we reached the sea, but we could not obtain a view of the ocean, although we made every endeavour to do so.* This is indeed crocodile country, and it may have been a good thing that they decided to turn around without actually wetting their feet in the waters of the Gulf.

On 22 December 1860, Burke, Wills, King and Gray arrived at Sturt's Stony Desert, which Wills described in his journal as nothing more or less than stony rises that we had before met with, only on a larger scale, and not quite as undulating . . . we thought it far from bad travelling ground.

Aboriginal people survived in this
country for tens of thousands of
years before European
settlement; some of the early
European explorers didn't fare so
well. It helps to know what to
eat and where to find it.
Mangrove worms (Toredo sp.)
taste a bit like oysters—if you
close your eyes.

The two men wasted no time, returning almost immediately to Camp 119 to collect King, Gray and the camels and begin the long haul back to the Cooper. It was now nearly two months since they'd left Cooper Creek, and they'd eaten well over half of their provisions. To get back to the depot they'd have to cross about 1100 kilometres, the first part mostly boggy ground. Through March and April 1861, the party stumbled through the mud and humidity, low on provisions and desperately weary. As the animals succumbed to the trying conditions, they were slaughtered and eaten. Gray's health deteriorated rapidly; one day Wills caught him sneaking some extra flour to eat and reported the incident to Burke. Burke thrashed Gray and accused him of malingering. That must have been the sort of leadership technique Burke learned back in the Old Country, as in, 'Give the men a good flogging every now and again—they like a good flogging'.

On 17 April, just four days short of Cooper Creek, Charlie Gray dropped down dead. It took a whole day for the other men to dig a shallow grave in the stony ground and bury his body. As things turned out, that day was to be a very expensive one.

But their bad luck was about to grow worse. At about 7.30 pm on Sunday 21 April, the three men arrived back at the Cooper Creek Depot to find it absolutely deserted—all the men and animals had gone. It was no wonder really, seeing Burke and his men were now a month overdue. Looking around, Wills found a message carved into the giant coolabah tree that overlooked the depot:

DIG

3FT. N.W.

APR. 21 1861

Following these instructions, the men dug down a couple of feet and found a box of rations and a message in a bottle. The message read:

Depot, Cooper's Creek, 21 April 1861,

The depot party of the VEE leaves this camp today to return to the Darling. I intend to go S.E. from Camp LX, to get into our old track near Bulloo. Two of my companions and myself are quite well; the third—Patton—has been unable to walk for the last eighteen days, as his leg has been severely hurt when thrown by one of the horses. No person has

The Queensland mud crab is one of my favourite foods. It's a pity that none of the early European explorers knew of its existence.

been up here from the Darling.

We have six camels and twelve horses in good working condition.

William Brahe.

So there's the twist—after waiting one month longer than Burke had asked him to, with no back-up supplies being brought from the Darling, Brahe had finally pulled the pin and departed—on the very same day that Burke and his men returned. Talk about events conspiring against you! Had they arrived back at the depot just one day earlier, history would have been different, but it was not to be.

That old coolabah tree is still out at Cooper Creek, and you can just make out Brahe's 'DIG' message carved into the heartwood of its massive trunk.

The 'Dig Tree'—a giant coolibah on the banks of Cooper Creek—is a lasting reminder of the Burke and Wills expedition. Nowadays a protective boardwalk, constructed by the Australian Army, surrounds the tree.

Before William Brahe and his
Depot party left Camp 65 at
Cooper Creek in April 1861,
they carved an inscription into
the heartwood of this tree. You
can still make out the 'Dig' part
of Brahe's message that
instructed Burke, Wills and King
how to find the supplies that
were left behind.

By the time Alfred Howitt's rescue party reached Cooper Creek, Burke and Wills were dead and King was only just alive, thanks to the kindness and hospitality of the local Aboriginal people.

Wills wrote in his journal,

Brahe has fortunately left us ample provisions to take us to the bounds of civilization, namely: flour, 50 lb; rice 20 lb, oatmeal 60 lb, sugar 60 lb and dried meat 15 lb. These provisions, together with a few horseshoes and nails, and some castaway odds and ends, constitute all the articles left, and place us in a very awkward position in respect to clothing.

And he went on to share more of their feelings:

Our disappointment at finding the depot deserted may easily be imagined; returning in an exhausted state, after four months of the severest travelling and privation, our legs almost paralysed, so that each of us found it a most trying task only to walk a few yards. Such a leg-bound feeling I never before experienced and hope I never shall again. The exertion required to get up a slight piece of rising ground, even without any load, induces an indescribable sensation of pain and helplessness, and the general lassitude makes one unfit for anything. Poor Gray must have suffered very much, many times, when we thought him shamming.

Well, after a bit of a feed and a good night's rest, the three men set out with the two remaining camels. Strangely they didn't follow Brahe's party. Instead they went in the opposite direction—south-west towards Mount Hopeless and Adelaide. Burke believed they had no chance of catching up with Brahe, and Mount Hopeless was much closer than the Menindee depot. What he didn't know was that to the south-west, Cooper Creek breaks up into smaller and smaller channels which eventually peter out into rocks, sandhills and waterless plains.

Two weeks after leaving the depot they were down to their last camel and Wills wrote,

The present state of things is not calculated to raise our spirits much. The rations are rapidly diminishing; our clothing, especially the boots, are all going to pieces, and we have not the materials for repairing them properly; the camel is completely done up, and can scarcely get along, although he has the best of feed and is resting half the time. I suppose this will end in our having to live like the blacks for a few months.

It's a pity they left it so late. The men had finally realised that their survival would depend on the hospitality of the local Aboriginal people. This in turn would call for a change in attitude. Suddenly the locals were no longer the mean-spirited, contemptible

This little fern, nardoo, contains thiaminase, an enzyme that attacks vitamin B1 in the body and stops you from digesting food. Aboriginal people knew how to detoxify the plant, but Burke and Wills succumbed to the effects of the poison and eventually died.

race that Wills had described in his journal before. Instead the explorers welcomed their gifts of food and even pituri, carefully prepared leaves of *Duboisia hopwoodii*, a desert plant found growing in the local area. King described just what it was like to chew on:

> *After chewing it for a few minutes I felt quite happy and perfectly indifferent about my position, in fact much the same effect as might be produced by two pretty stiff nobblers of brandy.*

Abandoning their efforts to reach Mount Hopeless, the men moved into an unoccupied gunyah and Wills set off to learn what he could about survival in the Cooper Creek region. One thing soon became apparent; during this season, the local Aborigines were largely dependent on a plant called nardoo. This plant is a fern which belongs to the *Marsilea* genus. Its seeds, or rather spores, lie dormant in the ground during droughts and spring up after rain. The nardoo fern grows to about 15 centimetres high, producing masses of little spores. By grinding and winnowing the spores, the Aborigines made a flour which they'd mix with water to form a paste. The paste was made into cakes which were baked in the fire.

The local Aborigines helped the explorers and gave them food whenever they could spare any. But the Aborigines would leave their camps for days at a time, and then the three men would be forced to look after themselves. They still made no attempt to shoot animals or to fish. In those days, the Cooper formed one of the most important trade routes for Australian Aborigines. In order for these hunter-gatherer societies to survive in such a harsh environment, a strict code of behaviour was followed. Daily activities were based on myths and rituals; individuals shared fairly the available food and resources.

While the state of the explorers' health slowly deteriorated, the Aboriginal people around them were thriving. Considering they were more or less eating the same food, this has been a bit of a mystery for some time. On 20 June 1861, Wills wrote

I cannot understand this nardoo at all—it certainly will not agree with me in any form; we are now reduced to it alone, and we manage to consume from four to five pounds per day between us; it appears to be quite indigestible, and cannot possibly be sufficiently nutritious to sustain life by itself.

Well, a few years ago, a really interesting scientific paper came up with a possible explanation. For tens of thousands of years, Aboriginal people in this area would gather nardoo spores and process them according to a strict ritual before eating them. Recent examination of the nardoo spores has revealed that they contain thiaminase, an enzyme that attacks vitamin B1 and prevents digestion. Because the explorers weren't preparing the nardoo the right way, they were gradually starving themselves.

On 29 June, Wills made his last journal entry, giving a final, accurate description of their predicament:

Nothing now but the greatest good luck can save any of us; and as for myself I may live four or five days if the weather continues warm. My pulse is at forty-eight, and very weak, and my legs and arms are nearly skin and bone. I can only look out, like Mr Micawber, 'for something to turn up'; starvation on nardoo is by no means very unpleasant, but for the weakness one feels, and the utter inability to move one's self; for as far as the appetite is concerned, it gives the greatest satisfaction. Certainly fat and sugar would be more to one's taste; in fact those seem to me to be the great stand-by for one in this extraordinary

Nardoo (Marsilea drummondii) is a type of fern that springs up after rain in the Cooper Creek area. The local Aborigines made flour from the spores of this plant that formed an important part of their diet. Had Burke and Wills paid more attention to the way the Aborigines prepared this bush tucker for eating, they probably would have survived to tell their tale.

continent: not that I mean to depreciate the farinaceous food; but the want of sugar and fat in all substances obtainable here is so great that they become almost valueless to us as articles of food, without the addition of something else.

Burke set up Camp 65, his Cooper Creek Depot, on the northern bank of a magnificent stretch of water full of fish and fresh water mussels. The mussels, along with nardoo, fish and other game, formed a staple diet for the Aboriginal people who were camped in the area.

In March, 1861, when no news had been heard from the Victorian Exploring Expedition for over five months, questions were raised by the Melbourne press. The Committee had been taking the approach that 'no news is good news', but with local journalists and Wills's father hot on their heels, it was time for action.

An experienced explorer by the name of Alfred Howitt offered to lead a light party to search for the missing expedition. His offer was accepted, and before the end of June Howitt met up with Brahe, who was on his way back to Melbourne. The Committee was right: no news was good news—Brahe's news was bad: Burke, Wills, King and Gray had been missing since 16 December, and four others had died.

But there was another twist to the story. After Brahe had left the Cooper Creek depot for Menindee, he'd met up with Wright and the rearguard near Bulloo. Wright was finally bringing up the much-needed stores, men and animals. Brahe and Wright decided to double back to Cooper Creek to see if there was any sign of the explorers. Arriving on 8 May they found the camp deserted and apparently untouched. On the very same day, Burke, Wills and King were just 50 kilometres away. They had already been to the depot and taken off on their short-lived attempt to get back to Melbourne. So they had missed Brahe a second time; this was fast becoming a Gilbert and Sullivan production, but with tragic results.

Howitt and Brahe returned to Melbourne to let the Committee members know the latest news. Howitt geared up for a full-scale rescue, while the Melbourne *Age* published a scathing report:

> *The unexpected news of Mr Burke's expedition of discovery, which we publish this morning, is positively disastrous. The entire company of explorers has been dissipated out of being, like dewdrops before the sun. Some are dead, some are on their way back. One has come to Melbourne, and another has made his way to Adelaide, whilst only four of the whole party have gone forward from the depot at Cooper's Creek upon the main journey of the expedition to explore the remote interior . . . The whole expedition appears to have been one prolonged blunder throughout; and it is to be hoped that the rescuing party may not be mismanaged and retarded in the same way as the unfortunate original expedition was.*

News of the disaster soon spread to the other colonies, and within a month or two, four separate parties had set off for the interior: two from Queensland, one from Adelaide and Howitt's team from Melbourne. Petty jealousies and intercolonial rivalry over exploration had given way to firm cooperation. Funnily enough, the efforts of those search parties provide us with a positive ending to the otherwise sad and sorry saga of Burke and Wills. The searchers explored huge tracts of previously unknown land, discovering new pastoral country and opening up new areas for settlement, all without the loss of life. Each of the rescue parties was led by an experienced explorer; all chose to travel light; and it was winter—the right time to be heading inland. It's interesting to think that these rescue parties were all manned by people with the right qualifications and background, and any one of them could have carried out the task that Burke and Wills had tried to achieve. But they weren't asked by the Melbourne-based committee, were they?

Not surprisingly, Howitt's party was the first to reach Cooper Creek, arriving at the Dig tree on 13 September. Unfortunately he was a bit late; Burke and Wills were dead, and King was only just alive, thanks to the kindness and hospitality of the local Aboriginal people.

The strangest thing about the whole debacle is that Burke almost pulled it off. You've really got to admire the courage, grit and determination of the men who made it all the way from Cooper Creek, almost to the Gulf and back again. And William John Wills proved himself a first class navigator.

*John McDouall Stuart knew
exactly what leadership was all
about. As his assistant Mr Auld
said,* There is nothing that
touches one more than the
remembrance of the deeds of
a truly brave man. We have
had the honour of having
served one. Ill as he was, the
agonies he suffered, still on he
went for the sake of his
party's safety . . . Stuart was
the king of Australian
explorers.

CHAPTER FIVE

JOHN MCDOUALL STUART

JOHN McDOUALL STUART has got to be Australia's number one explorer. He's the Scottish bloke who, back in the early 1860s, finally opened up a 3000 kilometre pathway from Adelaide through the centre of Australia and right up to the north coast. It was a tremendous feat of exploration, and what's more the whole team made it back alive.

I find Stuart's courage, determination and bushmanship really inspiring. But for me, the most interesting thing about his journeys is the detail he noted down along the way—small things he saw and encountered. And some of it, even today, is still a mystery. I think it's worth having a closer look

at Stuart—the sort of man he was and the way he went about his job of exploration.

When he was just a wee lad back in Scotland, Stuart faced a couple of tough challenges in life: being sent off to school at the Scottish Naval and Military Academy in Edinburgh, and the separate deaths of both his parents. From an early age he learned discipline and self-reliance. He went on to become a civil engineer, but never really settled down.

When Stuart was in his early 20s, the British Government was promoting the idea of migrating to the Australian colonies. South Australia was the place to go, they reckoned. It was the youngest colony, and the only one to be settled without convicts. Public notices were calling for 'young men and women with courage and ambition' to go and try their luck in a land of opportunities.

With no reason to stay in Scotland, Stuart jumped on a ship in 1838 and made the four month voyage to South Australia. Adelaide, an isolated settlement on the Gulf of Saint Vincent, was pretty rough and ready in those days. Most of the settlers were living in wooden huts with dirt floors and thatched roofs, built among thick eucalypt scrub. There were no roads—just dirt tracks.

As the young colony was facing a shortage of food and money, the South Australian Government wanted to encourage settlers to move out of the city and establish pastoral leases. But first the land had to be surveyed, and surveyors were in short supply. Stuart was more than happy to sign up. Conditions in the outback survey camps were fairly basic, but it was all new to him and there was plenty to learn. Life in the bush was pretty exciting, and Stuart stayed with the job until the early 1840s, when the government closed down his camp.

Stuart first explored Australia with Captain Charles Sturt in 1844, but the Simpson Desert proved to be an impenetrable barrier to their goal.

His next big adventure was to join a major expedition into Australia's unknown interior in 1844, under command of the respected explorer, Captain Charles Sturt. The expedition had two specific goals: to locate the geographical centre of Australia and to search for an inland sea. The Simpson Desert stopped them in their tracks, but Stuart was inspired by the vast expanse of *terra incognita*. He learned a lot from Sturt, particularly about methods of exploration, the nature of the inland country and, most importantly, how to survive there. He was determined to have another go, but he'd have to wait.

Back in Adelaide, Stuart became pretty restless. He was a quiet, down-to-earth bloke with a big bushy beard—a fair dinkum bachelor who didn't get into city life or socialising. So he headed back to the bush, where he earned his keep as a prospector and private survey contractor. This line of work led him to meet James Chambers and William Finke, a couple of local graziers.

By the late 1850s, five colonies had been established in Australia: New South Wales, Van Diemen's Land, Western Australia, South Australia and Victoria. A network of telegraph lines linked the far-flung areas of settlement, but there was no connection with overseas lines. News from the rest of the world arrived by ship—a few months later. There was talk of building a transcontinental line from Adelaide to the north coast, where it could hook into a submarine cable already linking Java with Europe. There was just one problem: no one had managed to cross the continent.

Well, the money-earning potential of this idea wasn't lost on the colonial governments, and before long the South Australians got pretty serious about wanting to find a way through to the north. But where to start?

In 1858, the South Australian Government decided to offer rewards for discoveries of new grazing land. William Finke contracted Stuart to explore the country west of Lake Torrens, an excellent proposal as it turned out. Stuart found over 60 000 square kilometres of pastoral country, earning himself a gold watch from the Royal Geographical Society and a grant of land from the government—anywhere he liked. Eventually he settled on grazing land about 600 kilometres north-north-west of Adelaide. Now known as Stuart Creek, he named his station Chambers Creek and used it as a base camp for future expeditions.

Before long he set out on another exploring journey, this time backed by Finke and Chambers. He headed north, discovering more pastoral country and, significantly, a series of 'mound springs' that really impressed him because, as he recorded: *I can go from here to Adelaide at any time of the year, and in any sort of season.* (What he didn't know was that the springs are natural outlets for the Great Artesian Basin, an enormous reserve of groundwater that lies beneath the dry plains. The springs, which for thousands of years provided Aborigines with reliable water, run along the basin's eastern edge between today's townships of Marree and Oodnadatta.)

By this time, plans for the Overland Telegraph Line were really hotting up. With Victoria also interested in winning the construction contract, the South Australian Government came up with another bright idea. It offered a reward of £2000 to the first person who could cross the continent from south to north. Guess who put his hand up for the job?

By now Stuart was an experienced explorer. He was quick to learn from the mistakes of others and this helped him develop his own method of exploration. His priorities were speed and mobility, and he reckoned the best way of achieving these was on horseback, accompanied by a team of packhorses. Without the drays, carts and 'moving stock' on which most of the other explorers relied, Stuart was forced to limit his supplies and equipment to the carrying capacity of his horses: about 120 pounds apiece.

Expedition rations consisted of dried meat, flour, tea, sugar and a bit of tobacco. Equipment included guns, ammunition, horseshoes, some tools and instruments, cooking pots, and a few waterbags. Only one tent was carried, and that was for Stuart to use in case of rain, so he could write up his notes and plan the next day's course.

There's no doubt that John McDouall Stuart could pick a good path. It's about as straight a line as you could hope for, allowing for the need to find water and to avoid really difficult terrain. Remember he wasn't just trying to cross the continent from south to north; he had to find a way that the telegraph line construction teams could follow. They would need reliable water supplies, and plenty of trees for making telegraph poles.

The only instruments he used were a sextant and artificial horizon for calculating his position, a prismatic compass for keeping his course, and a hand-held telescope. He had one map: a copy of Matthew Flinders's chart, such as it was, of the north coast of Australia. As this chart showed only the coastline and a few of the river mouths, it wasn't much use to him for 90 per cent of his journey.

Stuart was aiming for the Victoria River, which the Gregory brothers had discovered a few years earlier. They'd followed the Victoria River and Sturt Creek from the north coast down to latitude 20°16' south, so Stuart reckoned if he could make it to that point he'd be home and hosed. But in between lay kilometres and kilometres of unknown land.

Stuart started off by doing a few mini-expeditions, each time pushing a bit further north—like a reconnaissance I guess. He found that the country around Lake Eyre was mostly desert. His previous discovery of the Great Artesian Basin's mound springs enabled him to cross the dry plains of the Douglas, Neales and Finke Rivers.

But more challenges lay ahead: gibber plains covered in red and yellow stones (a real hassle to walk across), then the range country where the James, Waterhouse and MacDonnell Ranges rise from the plains. Each range is a series of parallel ridges running east-west. Between the ridges are lush, grassy valleys, but the rivers don't flow along the valleys—they cut across them. If you're wondering how this could be, it's because the rivers were there way before the ranges.

North of the MacDonnells a vast plain stretches for hundreds of kilometres, occasionally broken by a few low ranges. Water can be hard to find, but after heavy rain temporary lakes form. As they dry up, deep cracks split the ground. Soon afterwards the grass springs up and hides the cracks; this can make walking a difficult task.

Further north there's no water at all on the plains—just sandhills and pockets of dense scrub. Then at about the 16th parallel, the northern tropics start. Deep, fast-flowing rivers like the Roper, which is lined with palm trees in places and thick, tangled scrub in others, alternate with boggy swamps and rough, broken mountain ranges. These eventually give way to the mudflats and mangroves that border the north coast.

This was Stuart's exploring technique: head off in the direction of travel, in this instance north-west. Look at the landscape—rocks, soil, vegetation, minerals and the lie of the land. Head for the highest bit of local ground with telescope, diary and compass to take note of the key geographical features, keeping an eye open for possible water catchments. Then quietly mull over all this information and plot the next leg of the journey.

In March 1860 John McDouall Stuart set out with William Kekwick, Benjamin Head and 13 horses to cross the Australian continent. For the first part of the journey they travelled over familiar ground, following the line of mound springs. Patchy rainfall made the ground boggy in places, but otherwise the going was pretty good.

A few weeks into the journey they struck their first problem: the horse that was carrying the instruments broke loose and threw its load. Unfortunately the sextant was damaged and *put out of adjustment*, as Stuart noted in his journal. It took him all day to repair and he couldn't be sure if it was fixed or not. Unfortunately there was no Global Positional System (GPS) back in those days.

That night heavy rain fell, soaking some of their provisions. Stuart was anxious to dry them out again, but it was a few days before the rain stopped, by which time he found *a quantity of our dried meat is quite spoiled, which is a great loss—another wet day and we should have lost the half of it.*

Just before the Neales River, the expedition struck scrubby mulga country which really slowed them down. *I can scarcely see one hundred yards before me,* Stuart wrote. *It is far worse than guiding a vessel at sea; the compass requires to be constantly in hand.* He changed course to the west, where the scrub was replaced by spinifex and sandhills. The men spent a whole day repairing their packs and bags, which had been badly torn by the mulga.

With rain continuing on and off, finding water was not a problem. However, they lost another day's travel, this time re-shoeing all the horses. The old horseshoes had been cut by the sharp stones of the gibber plains. Stuart was an excellent horseman and was well aware of the need to care for his animals; without them the expedition would come to a grinding halt.

By nature Stuart was not a man to complain, but every now and then he had a quiet whinge in his journal, usually about his health. By the time they got to the Stevenson River, he was starting to have a real problem with his eyesight:

I find to-day that my right eye, from the long continuation of bad eyes, is now become useless to me for taking observations. I now see two suns instead of one, which has led me into an error of a few miles. I trust to goodness my other eye will not become the same; as long as it remains good, I can do.

Stuart put this problem down to the glare of the sun, but it's more likely that he was suffering from sandy blight, or trachoma as the medicos call it. Sandy blight is a

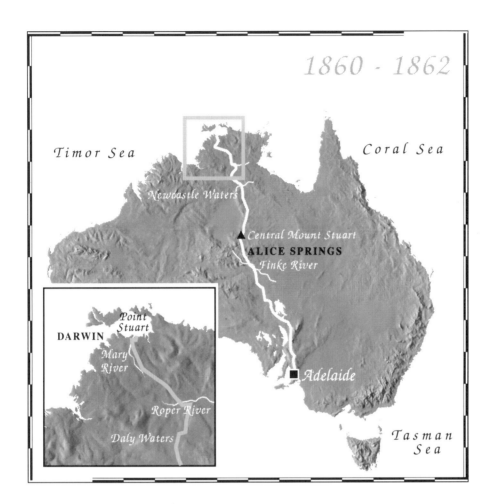

terrible eye disease—a form of conjunctivitis that, without treatment, can lead to blindness. It's quite common in dry conditions, particularly where there's a combination of heat, dust, low humidity and bright sunlight. Sounds just like Australia's desert country.

One of the best things about being an explorer, apart from discovering new places, is that you get to name them. In Stuart's case, he mostly honoured his sponsors and friends, or people in high positions of government. It was his way of saying thanks for the help he'd been given. The Finke River and Chambers Pillar are two of the hundreds of places Stuart named during his journeys.

Before the expedition had reached the MacDonnell Ranges, *the first real range since leaving the Flinders*, deep ravines and dense scrub slowed their progress and shredded clothing and saddle-bags. Flies tormented them and the symptoms of scurvy were beginning to show.

On 22 April 1860 Stuart
named 'Central Mount Sturt' in
honour of his mentor and former
boss, Captain Charles Sturt, but
the mapmakers later changed the
name to Central Mount Stuart
in honour of the man himself.

Scurvy is a terrible disease. It had been rife in the outback survey camps, so Stuart was no stranger to it. It's caused by a deficiency of vitamin C and is quickly cured if you've got access to fresh food, particularly fruit and vegetables. As it was imperative for the expedition to move quickly, there was no time to wander off and look for bush tucker. Now and again the men would find a bit of portulaca or saltbush, or they might even shoot a bird for the pot.

Another problem with a fast-moving expedition is that there's no time for scientific study. In those days most of the explorers took a scientist or two along, whose job was to catalogue the plants and animals and so on, and to collect specimens. In Stuart's case this pastime would have seriously hindered progress, so the plants and animals were spared to some degree, although plant collecting was undertaken from time to time.

On 22 April Stuart achieved one of his long-held ambitions. He wrote in his journal, *Today I find from my observations of the sun, 111°00′30″, that I am now camped in the centre of Australia*. It was a simple statement, but I bet he was thrilled. In memory of his former boss and mentor, he named the nearest mountain Central Mount Sturt. But later, when he got back to Adelaide, the Parliament and map-makers changed it round. They called it Central Mount Stuart, which is probably much more appropriate.

These days, with technology and satellites, we've found out that the centre of the Australian continent is about 400 kilometres to the south. But in Stuart's time a couple of books had published maps that marked the supposed centre of the continent around the area of Central Mount Sturt. No doubt Stuart was influenced by them when he picked his location, and when you think about it, it's taken us another hundred years to correct the fault, so we can't be too hard on him.

Out on the spinifex plains in early May, Stuart was wishing he'd turned back earlier. His main problem was a shortage of water. The expedition was well and truly in *terra incognita*, and with all those horses, finding water was the first priority. While he was out looking one day, he made a very interesting observation:

the track of the native was peculiar—not broad and flat, as they generally are, but long and narrow, with a deep hollow in the foot, and the large toe projecting a good deal; the other in some respects more like the print of a white man than of a native.

The expedition hadn't encountered many Aboriginal people, but that was about to change.

A little later, to their great relief, they came across a 'native well'. Many of these wells are formed by rocky depressions in the ground that catch and hold rainwater. Quite often the Aborigines would cover the openings with large, flat stones to stop the water from evaporating. In this instance, the well that Stuart found was a sandy one, more like a dug-out soak in a shallow depression or creek bed. Such wells are generally fairly small and contain only a few gallons of water; but in that part of the world it can mean the difference between life and death.

Next morning at daybreak, Stuart went to the well for a drink and was horrified to see:

the rascals of horses had been there before us, and trodden in one side of the well. They had as much water last night and morning as they could drink, and the quantity that some of them drank was enormous. I had no idea that a horse could hold so much, yet still they want more.

From there on, things started to go downhill. Both men and horses were losing condition and by mid-May Stuart was plagued by scurvy:

my hands are a complete mass of sores that will not heal . . . My mouth and gums are now so bad that I am obliged to eat flour and water boiled. The pains in my limbs and muscles are almost insufferable.

It's a real testament to his determination that he continued the journey. By the following night he felt so bad he reckoned he almost wished he was dead. His muscles were turning black and he could barely swallow anything at all. The main problem, Stuart realised, was that his team was too small.

After a short rest they pressed on to the north, through the range country. In the spinifex plains round Tennant Creek, Stuart made another interesting note: *we crossed some marks very much resembling old horse-tracks.*

Now this is one of those interesting details that are rather difficult to explain, although it has been suggested that the horse tracks could have resulted from Leichhardt's passing through the area en route from Moreton Bay to Swan River in 1848—that is

*During his first attempts to reach
either the Victoria River or the
far north coast, Stuart was
defeated by the parched plains
north of Newcastle Waters.
These days much of that country
is taken up by cattle properties,
like Newcastle Waters station,
pictured here.*

*Crossing the Roper River proved
to be a major challenge for
Stuart. Looking for the best
place to get across one of his
horses drowned.*

certainly a possibility. Another possibility is that the horse tracks were left by straying stock moving west from Sydney or north from South Australia, or perhaps by some other explorer that we know nothing about.

Things picked up for Stuart and his men until the second week in June, just south of Bishop Creek, when three of the horses could barely walk. They had now been over four days without a drop of water and Stuart was forced to *leave as many things at this camp as I could possibly do without*. From then on, he was to have some very interesting encounters with the local Aborigines.

On 20 June, John McDouall Stuart named Kekwick Ponds for his second-in-command, *in token of the zeal and activity he has displayed during the expedition*. The ponds are actually a series of small waterholes, all quite shallow, but very welcome in such arid country. During the wet season, they tend to spread out and link together. In fact it's one of the very few places in Central Australia where I've seen waterlilies (*Nymphaea* sp) growing; they give the area a very special charm all of its own. I can really understand why Stuart and his crew were so attracted to the place.

Even these days the spearheads and chippings lying around are evidence that Kekwick Ponds was once an occupation site for Aboriginal people. Well, Stuart reckoned he was down by one of the waterways one day when a small group of Aborigines came up, three or four of them, including an old man. He said he stood there looking at them, giving them signs to come across and have a feed if they wanted to, or a drink of water. They didn't do anything for a while, and then they surprised him. What happened, he said, was that the old man gave him one of the 'masonic signs'—whatever that may be. Stuart didn't believe his eyes. He just stood there watching and watching and they did it again—all three of them repeated it. And he answered them—with a masonic sign, I suppose.

You've got to remember that back in those days, a lot of the explorers were members of the Masonic Lodge, so Stuart presumably knew exactly what he was doing—and what the Aborigines were doing for that matter. Anyway, once he gave them the sign, they all came across and patted him on the back—reckoned he was a good bloke and all the rest of it. Then off they went. You can read about this incident in Stuart's journal. It's a pretty strange thing to have happened, particularly when you consider that Stuart and his men were supposedly the first white people to have travelled through that part of the country.

What on earth were Aborigines in Central Australia doing with masonic signs? It's puzzling stuff. But it's the areas north of Kekwick Ponds that I find really fascinating.

Stuart was very interested in Aboriginal people. But he was also careful not to

annoy them in any way. He was aware that some of Leichhardt's men had been speared further north, and he feared that there could be *far worse in advance of us*. As it turned out, he wasn't too far wide of the mark.

The men were looking for water again on 26 June when:

we saw where they had been examining our tracks, and as we approached the creek their tracks became very numerous on ours. When we arrived on the top of the rise, where we had previously seen their camp and fires, we could now see nothing of them, neither smoke, fires, nor anything else: it was then nearly dark.

Next minute, without warning, the local Aborigines—the Warramunga people— attacked. These were the same people who, three or four days ago back at Kekwick Ponds, had given Stuart the masonic sign. He tells us that they ambushed him—a perfect ambush, he reckoned. *If they had been Europeans they could not better have arranged and carried out their plan of attack.*

But the really strange thing is, the Warramunga didn't throw any spears. Instead, all they threw were boomerangs. Basically I think what they were doing was saying, 'Hey get out of here, go away, we don't want you here. This is our water, there's not

much of it and you're drinking it all. Clear out'. I don't think this was an attack in the real sense of the word, but rather a bit of a local warning. Even so, the creek where the incident occurred is still named Attack Creek.

At the end of the whole thing, Stuart makes a very, very interesting comment in his journal about these Warramunga people. He says, *I think they must have seen or encountered white men before.*

Stuart was now quite ill, and his men and horses were exhausted. Rations were low, very little rain had fallen in the past few months, and the Aborigines were still close by. Being concerned for the safety of his men, he decided to return all the way back to Adelaide, a journey of 2000 kilometres.

They arrived back in October to a heroes' welcome; the local press described Stuart as the 'Napoleon of explorers', and for his *discretion, prudence and courage*, the

Stuart's initial attempts to cross the Australian continent were thwarted by a shortage of water.

Royal Geographical Society awarded him their Patron's Medal, the highest honour an explorer could receive.

By this time the Burke and Wills expedition from Victoria was well on its way north. To the competitive colonies, the only real concern for the moment was who should be first to the coast. With this in mind, the South Australian Parliament voted to sponsor Stuart to the tune of £2500 on another attempt. At the end of November he left Adelaide with seven men and 30 horses, heading for Chambers Creek. There they got themselves organised: killing and drying bullocks, shoeing horses, repairing saddles and bags, weighing rations and so on. By the time they were ready, they'd gained another five men and had a total of 49 horses.

After the first week of travel, five of the horses had packed it in. To balance this out, Stuart calculated he'd have to send two of his men back with a month's worth of supplies. That would leave him with ten men, 45 horses and 30 weeks' provisions.

He pretty well followed his old track north, reaching the Finke River by late February. Two months later, the party again reached Attack Creek. Stuart kept a mile to the west of his old track, where the country was more open. I guess he was a bit nervous about stirring up the Warramunga people again.

A little further north at Tomkinson Creek, Kekwick was looking for water one morning when he reckoned he found some wheat growing. Now in 1861, I find that quite extraordinary. Stuart must have been wondering if he really was the first European to visit this area. Here in Australia, wheat does not grow naturally, and we have absolutely nothing that could possibly be mistaken for wheat, yet both Kekwick and Stuart both felt that they had stumbled across wheat growing way out in the middle of the continent. Stuart noted in his journal that it:

> very much resembles wheat in straw (which is very tough), ear, and seed. It grows two feet high. The seed is small, but very much like wheat both in shape and colour.

From bases there and at Newcastle Waters a little further north, the expedition tried and tried to break through to the Victoria River. It lay just 225 kilometres to the north-west, but the dry, scrubby country, intense heat and a shortage of supplies finally defeated them.

On location for ABC TV, filming a piece-to-camera.

Stuart wrote on 11 July:

We have now run out of everything. We are all nearly naked, the scrub has been so severe on our clothes; one can scarcely tell the original colour of a single garment, everything is so patched. Our boots are also gone. It is with great reluctance that I am forced to return.

In September 1861, only a day or so after Stuart's arrival in Adelaide, regardless of his need to rest and recover his health, he offered to try again. The government accepted and voted to equip another expedition. This time he was to have everything he desired, but his preoccupation with weight kept the list simple. By now news of the deaths of Burke and Wills at Coopers Creek had filtered back to Adelaide.

In less than a month, Stuart had got himself organised. He took Mr Kekwick (2nd officer), Mr Thring (3rd officer), Mr Auld (assistant), a blacksmith, a saddler and four other men. Mr Waterhouse was signed on as naturalist at the government's insistence. They would be accompanied by a total of 71 horses.

As usual, the first big stop was Chambers Creek, to cut and dry beef for the trip and to weigh and number packs. Stuart was now a professional explorer and absolutely determined to succeed. This time he was leaving nothing to chance. He drew up a set of rules and circulated them amongst his men:

- All orders to proceed from the leader: in Stuart's absence, Kekwick would take charge, and should they both be gone, Thring.

- Officers were to ensure that orders were promptly and willingly obeyed and that the workload was evenly divided among the men.

- Any disobedience, disagreement, or neglect of duty was to be reported to Stuart immediately.

- Thring was in charge of the horses. No horse was to be abused, kicked, or struck about the head. Sore backs were to be attended to after unsaddling. No horse was to be put out of a walk unless absolutely necessary. The men were not to sit on the saddles unless riding.

- Kekwick was in charge of supplies and equipment; nothing was to be removed from any bag without his knowledge. Anything used was to be returned to its place exactly as it had been found. Each pair of bags was to be of equal weight.

- The watch was to be armed at all times and was to exercise the greatest vigilance. Anything, however insignificant, that caught his attention was to be reported to the leader immediately. In case of Aboriginal attack the men were to form a half-circle, with each man spaced three feet apart.

- The watch was to call the party at daybreak. Bedclothes were to be packed in their proper places; breakfast were to be ready and eaten in half an hour.

- Immediately after, the horses were to be brought in unhobbled; riding horses were to be saddled and loaded first.

- Leaving the line of march without the leader's knowledge was forbidden; no water was to be used from the canteens without permission.

- Leaving camp alone or without guns and ammunition was forbidden.

- Anyone detached on special duty from camp or the line of march was to report himself on return.

- Firing on Aborigines without orders was forbidden, unless in self-defence.

- Swearing, improper language, keeping journals and taking notes were forbidden.

- Scientific specimens were to be delivered to Mr Waterhouse.
- No rules were to be altered before consulting Stuart.

The most important rule of all was that when in camp, one man had to stand watch every two hours, day and night. Stuart threatened to shoot dead anyone found asleep on watch. Reading this list of rules and regulations, and knowing some of the problems he'd encountered in the past, I would say that Stuart was determined to eliminate any waste or inefficiency. He probably realised in his heart that this would be his last chance to make it to the Top End.

Thring's strategy with the horses was to divide them among the men, who then cared for the animals as if they owned them. When the party arrived at the camp-site, the packs were unloaded into four rows in numerical order, a system that enabled Kekwick to find what he wanted without trouble. The story goes that after a while the horses knew their rows and would form into a line.

According to Auld,

When every horse was packed we would mount, Stuart would light his pipe—he was very fond of his pipe—take a bearing with his prismatic compass, replace it in the case, and start.

The horses, some wearing bells, followed one behind the other.

By mid-April the expedition had reached Howells Ponds at the northern end of Newcastle Waters. This had been Stuart's farthest camp north on his last attempt. Here, in the intense heat, the real work started.

The men were on strict rations and Auld reckoned that:

The conversation of the party now consisted entirely in informing each other of the visions we had seen on the previous night. In every case the subject was the same. Dinner parties, going into restaurants and astonishing everyone by the quantities we ate, and then not being satisfied. This may not be romantic, but it is true. The food supplies troubled us sorely, and we were at considerable pains to replenish our poverty-stricken larder. In one time of extremity a nest of wild-dog pups was found. These innocents were slaughtered and boiled, and were eaten, and were delicious!

The only books they had to read were Bibles and a nautical almanac.

The Roper is one of the most impressive rivers in northern Australia, and one of my favourites. Named by Ludwig Leichhardt in September 1845 for his team mate, John Roper, the river runs for hundreds of kilometres and has a peacefulness that I feel is all its own.

They stayed at Howells Ponds for a month. During this time Stuart took small parties out to recce a way ahead. He was still trying to reach the Victoria River to link up with Gregory's route, but once again the Great Sandy Desert defeated him. Eventually he headed due north and found Daly Waters, which in turn led him to the Strangways River. From now on, as finding water was no longer a problem, the expedition rode north together.

If you ever happen to get up to Daly Waters, a kilometre or so behind the pub you can still see one of the trees that Stuart marked on his way north. The tree is old and dead now, but you can just make out the large capital letter S, carved into the grey wood of the tree trunk.

Towards the end of June they arrived at one of Australia's most beautiful rivers,

On 23 May, 1962, Stuart named Daly Waters pictured here during a dry spell. *Having seen what I consider to be permanent water, I shall now run a straight course, to see if the water continues.* The north-flowing series of waterholes led him to the Strangways River and from then on, finding water was no longer a problem.

Lilies (Nymphaea sp.) adorn waterholes adjacent to the Roper River.

When Stuart acompanied
Captain Charles Sturt on his
expedition to find the centre of
Australia, the Simpson Desert
stopped them in their tracks.

It really fascinates me that, if Lieutenant Nixon's report is correct, the Dutch shipwreck survivors moved so far from the coast before settling in Australia's interior. One day I hope to find remnants of their small colony, like this reminder of Victoria Settlement, a former British establishment at Port Essington on Cobourg Peninsula.

The Dutch shipwreck survivors who trekked inland from Australia's west coast would have crossed miles and miles of spinifex country like this. Spinifex, or porcupine grass, is unique to Australia. It grows from the centre outwards in clumps that can span up to 20 metres.

the Roper—*a splendid navigable river*. When John McDouall Stuart got to that point, he'd finished with the arid zone country. The Roper was the first real waterway he'd come up against, and finding a place to cross it caused the men and horses no end of trouble. Eventually they succeeded, but one of the horses fell in and drowned. Next day the horse was cut up and dried, to the men's delight:

This food supply made all hands happy, for we had three meals that day—meals, too, of freshly killed meat with native cucumbers as a relish. We thought that horse meat surpassed anything we had ever eaten.

But what a contrast! They'd gone from not enough water to too much, because from there on it's wetland country, all the way through to the Top End. They'd had very few encounters with the local Aborigines, but at the Roper River the locals responded to the intrusion by setting fire to the surrounding grass.

Once across the Roper, Stuart didn't muck around. They climbed some rough, stony hills to the top of a tableland:

When we had gone about 13 miles on the tableland we were suddenly stopped. We found ourselves on the edge of a precipice about two or three hundred feet. The scenery was simply grand.

The men were looking out over the Arnhem Land escarpment. Their last major obstacles were kilometres of stony ranges, wetlands and boggy ground. On 11 July Stuart finally found a river that he hoped would lead them to the coast, and he named it the Mary, *in honour of Mary Chambers.*

One night, a week or so later, Stuart and Auld calculated from their observations that they were just a few miles from the coast. After nine long, hard months they'd practically reached their goal. But Stuart wanted to surprise his men, and so that night he kept their position a secret.

As they hacked a path through the last of the vine thickets on 24 July 1862, they heard a sound that caused a great deal of excitement.

Thring, who rode in advance of me, called out 'The Sea!', which so took them all by surprise, and they were so astonished, that he had to repeat the call before they fully understood what was meant. Then they immediately gave three long and hearty cheers.

On 24 July 1862, John
McDouall Stuart and his team
finally reached the shores of Van
Diemen Gulf. Next day Stuart
recorded, I now had an open
place cleared, and selecting
one of the tallest trees,
stripped it of its lower
branches, and on its highest
branch fixed my flag, the
Union Jack, with my name
sewn in the centre of it.
When this was completed, the
party gave three cheers . . .

They rushed to the water's edge but held the horses back because of the soft sand and mud. Stuart washed his hands and feet in the sea, while his men collected shells. The next day they raised the Union Jack and gave three cheers for the Queen. After remaining on the coast for only two days, the party began its return. They were running desperately short of rations and scurvy had started to show.

The condition of the horses deteriorated rapidly, and at the Chambers River, a tributary of the Roper, Stuart ordered his men to leave behind everything they could do without, including boots and clothes, keeping only what they stood in. Poor old Waterhouse had to part with most of his valuable collection of specimens. So often this sort of sacrifice happened with these expeditions, but I guess when you weigh up the practicalities, it had to be done. Leichhardt had been faced with exactly the same dilemma a couple of years earlier.

Just north of Newcastle Waters, a group of Aboriginal people followed the expedition. *They are a fine race of men, tall, stout, and muscular,* Stuart observed, *They were 17 in number; four of them were boys, one of them much lighter than the others, nearly a light yellow.* Clearly Stuart was not the first white person to move through this part of the country.

Stuart himself was suffering more than any of his men—his health was shattered from almost four years of hard journeying. Not far south of Newcastle Waters he confided to his journal,

I am very doubtful of my being able to reach the settled districts. Should anything happen to me, I keep everything ready for the worst. My plan is finished, and my journal brought up every night.

Back at Attack Creek, Auld and Thring had a rather strange encounter with one of the locals—again it was one of the Warramunga people. The two men were washing some clothes about 200 metres from camp, when an Aboriginal man approached them. He talked and made signs, then untied Auld's bootlace and took off his boot and sock. Auld signalled him to replace them, which he did, tying the bootlace back in a bow just as he'd found it. Now I reckon that's pretty remarkable behaviour; something rather strange would appear to have been going on around there if you ask me.

As the expedition moved south, the waterholes were drying out fast, and weak as the men and horses were, it was imperative to move as quickly as possible. But Stuart's health continued to deteriorate until he could no longer walk or ride. The men made him a stretcher, which they slung between a couple of horses. For Stuart the movement was agonising, and sometimes when the men lifted him down at the end of a day's march they reckoned he looked more dead than alive.

In December 1862 they finally reached Adelaide, where they were treated like heroes—which of course they were. But for Stuart, the game was over. His health never really recovered and he sort of lost his way in life—lost his direction, his purpose. The South Australian Government had fleetingly considered giving him a knighthood, but that never happened. Four years after achieving his goal to cross the Australian

Crowds mobbed Stuart's expedition on its triumphant return to Adelaide.

continent, John McDouall Stuart was back in Pitstone Green just outside London—dead.

It's a sad ending, but I reckon the really interesting part about the whole expedition is the manpower. The same blokes kept coming back year after year, trying to break through to the coast. Obviously they enjoyed working with Stuart, and thoroughly respected him. As his assistant Mr Auld said,

There is nothing that touches one more than the remembrance of the deeds of a truly brave man. We have had the honour of having served one. Ill as he was, the agonies he suffered, still on he went for the sake of his party's safety. . . . Stuart was the king of Australian explorers.

There's no doubt that John McDouall Stuart knew exactly what leadership was all about. And as for all those strange things that happened along the way—well, perhaps we may be on the edge of cracking that one!

ORIGINAL ESSAY.

'SCOVERY OF A WHITE COLONY ON THE NORTHERN SHORE OF NEW HOLLAND.

A Correspondent living near Halifax has favoured us with e following interesting communication :—

TO THE EDITORS OF THE LEEDS MERCURY.

GENTLEMEN,—A friend of mine, lately arrived from ngapore, via India overland, having been one of a party who landed at Raffles Bay, on the north coast of New Holland, on the 10th of April, 1832, and made a two months' excursion into the interior, has permitted me to copy the following extract out of his private journal, which I think contains some particulars of a highly interesting nature, and not generally known.

The exploring party was promoted by a scientific Society at Singapore, aided and patronized by the Local Government, and its object was both commercial and geographical; but it was got up with the greatest secrecy and remained secret to all except the parties concerned. (For what good purpose it is impossible to conceive :—)

Extract from an unpublished manuscript Journal of an exploring party in Northern Australia, by Lieutenant Nixon.

" May 15th, 1832.—On reaching the summit of the hill, no words can express the astonishment, delight, and wonder I felt at the magical change of scenery, after having travelled for so many days over nothing but barren hills and rocks, and sands and parching plains, without seeing a single tribe of aborigines excepting those on the sea coast, and having to dig for water every day.

" Looking to the southwards, I saw below me, at the distance of about three or four miles, a low and level country, laid out as it were in plantations, with straight rows of trees, through which a broad sheet of smooth water extended in nearly a direct line from east to west, as far as the eye could reach to the westward, but apparently sweeping to the southward at its eastern extremity like a river; and near its banks, at one particular spot on the south side, there appeared to be a group of habitations, embosomed in a grove of tall trees like palms. The water I guessed to be about half a mile wide, and although the stream was clearly open for two thirds of the distance from the southern bank, the remainder of it was studded by thousands of little islands stretching along its northern shores : and what fixed me to the spot with indescribable sensations of rapture and admiration was the number of small boats or canoes with one or two persons in each, gliding along the narrow chanels between the little islands in every direction, some of which appeared to be fishing or drawing nets. None of them had a sail, but one that was floating down the body of the stream without wind, which seemed to denote that a current ran from east to west. It seemed as if enchantment had brought me into a civilized country, and I could scarcely resolve to leave the spot I stood upon, had it not been for the overpowering rays of a mid day sun, affecting

The Leeds Mercury, January 1834. This article claimed the discovery of a long-term Dutch settlement in northern New Holland.

CHAPTER SIX

THE DUTCH SETTLEMENT

ON 29 APRIL 1993, little did I realise what I was about to get myself into. I was talking to a mate of mine, Peter Gesner, a marine archaeologist, in his office at the Queensland Museum in Brisbane. We'd spent the morning examining some artefacts that had only recently been discovered on the ocean floor, among the decaying wreckage of the *Pandora*. Old bottles, surgical instruments and the like, these bits and pieces had remained undisturbed for hundreds of years. Over a cup of coffee, which we sat drinking on the museum balcony, our conversation drifted from the wreck of the *Pandora* to outside influences on Kimberley rock art. Suddenly Peter remembered he had

something that he thought might interest me in relation to early (pre-1788) settlement in northern Australia. It was an article that had been published in the *Leeds Mercury*, an English provincial newspaper, in 1834. This is how it ran:

DISCOVERY OF A WHITE COLONY ON THE NORTHERN SHORE OF NEW HOLLAND

A correspondent living near Halifax has favoured us with the following interesting communication:

TO THE EDITOR OF THE LEEDS MERCURY.

GENTLEMEN—

A friend of mine, lately arrived from Singapore, via India overland, having

I'll bet this sight of Cobourg
Peninsula was a welcome one to
the sailors who made their way
here in the early days of
European settlement. Sandy
beaches around the peninsula
offer safe anchorage and the
beautifully clear water is full of
mud crabs, fish, turtles, dugongs
and of course the odd saltwater
crocodile.

been one of a party who landed at Raffles Bay, on the north coast of New Holland, on
the 10th of April, 1832, and made a two months' excursion into the interior, has permitted
me to copy the following extract out of his private journal, which I think contains some
particulars of a highly interesting nature, and not generally known.

The exploring party was promoted by a scientific Society at Singapore, aided and
patronised by the Local Government and its object was both commercial and geographical;
but it was got up with the greatest secrecy, and remained secret to all except the parties
concerned (for what good purpose it is impossible to conceive).

Extract from an unpublished manuscript Journal of an exploring party in
Northern Australia by Lieutenant Nixon:

'May 15th, 1832.—On reaching the summit of the hill, no words can express the
astonishment, delight and wonder I felt at the magical change of scenery, after having
travelled for so many days over nothing but barren hills and rocks, and sands and parching
plains, without seeing a single tribe of aborigines excepting those on the sea coast and having
to dig for water every day.

'Looking to the southwards I saw below me at the distance of about three or four
miles, a low and level country, laid out as it were in plantations, with straight rows of
trees, through which a broad sheet of smooth water extended in nearly a direct line from
east to west, as far as the eye could reach to the westward, but apparently sweeping to
the southward at its eastern extremity like a river; and near its banks, at one particular
spot on the south side there appeared to be a group of habitations embosomed in a grove
of tall trees like palms.

'The water I guessed to be about half a mile wide, and although the stream was
clearly open for two thirds of the distance from the southern bank, the remainder of it was
studded by thousands of little islands stretching along its northern shores: and what fixed
me to the spot with indescribable sensations of rapture and admiration was the number of
small boats or canoes with one or two persons in each gliding along the narrow chanels
between the islands in every direction, some of which appeared to be fishing or drawing
nets. None of them had a sail, but one was floating down the body of the stream without
wind, which seemed to denote a current ran from east to west.

'It seemed as if enchantment had brought me to a civilised country, and I could scarcely resolve to leave the spot I stood upon, had it not been for the overpowering rays of a mid day sun affecting my bowels, as it frequently had done, during all the journey.

'On reaching the bottom of the hill, in my return to our party at the tents, I was just turning round a low rock, when I came suddenly upon a human being whose face was so fair and dress so white, that I was for a moment staggered with terror, and thought I was looking at an apparition. I had naturally expected to meet an Indian as black or as brown as the rest of the natives, and not a white man in these unexplored regions. Still quaking with doubts about the integrity of my eyes I proceeded on, and saw the apparition advancing upon me with the most perfect indifference: in another minute he was quite near, and I now perceived that he had not yet seen me, for he was walking slowly and pensively with his eyes fixed on the ground and he appeared to be a young man of handsome and interesting countenance.

'We were got within four paces of each other when he heaved a deep and tremulous sigh, raised his eyes, and in an instant uttered a loud exclamation and fell insensible to the ground. My fears had now given place to sympathy, and I hastened to assist the unknown, who I felt convinced, had been struck with the idea of seeing a supernatural being. It was considerable time before he recovered and was assured of my mortality; and from a few expressions in old Dutch which he uttered, I was luckily enabled to hold some conversation with him; for I had been at school in Holland in my youth and had not quite forgotten the language.

'Badly as he spoke Dutch, yet I gathered from him a few particulars of a most extraordinary nature; namely, that he belonged to a small community, all as white as himself, he said about three hundred; that they lived in houses enclosed all to-gether within a great wall to defend them from black men; that their fathers came there about one hundred and seventy years ago, as they said, from a distant land across the great sea; and that their ship broke, and eighty men and ten of their sisters (female passengers?) with many things were saved onshore.

'I prevailed on him to accompany me to my party, who I knew would be glad to be introduced to his friends before we set out on our return to our ship at Port Raffles, from which place we were now distant nearly five hundred miles, and our time was linked to a fixed period so as to enable the ship to carry us back to Singapore before the change of the monsoon. The young man's dress consisted of a round jacket and large breeches, both made of skins, divested of the hair and bleached as white as linen; and on his head he wore a tall white skin cap with a brim covered over with white down or the small feathers of the white cocatoo.

'The latitude of this mountain was eighteen degrees thirty mins fourteen secs south; and the longitude one hundred and thirty two degrees twenty five minutes thirty seconds east. It was christened Mount Singapore, after the name and in honour of the settlement to which the expedition belonged.'

A subsequent part of the journal states further,

'that on our party visiting the white village, the joy of the simple inhabitants was quite extravagant. The descendant of an officer is looked up to as chief, and with him (whose name is Van Baerle) the party remained eight days. Their traditional history is that their fathers were compelled by famine, after the loss of their great vessel, to travel towards the rising sun, carrying with them as much of the stores as they could, during which many died; and by the wise advice of their ten sisters they crossed a ridge of land, and meeting with a rivulet on the other side, followed its course and were led to the spot they now inhabit, where they have continued ever since.

'They have no animals of the domestic kind, either cows, sheep, pigs or anything else. Their plantations consist only of maize and yams, and these with fresh and dried fish constitute their principal food, which is changed occasionally for Kangaroo and other game; but it appears that they frequently experience a scarcity and shortage of provisions, most probably owing to ignorance and mismanagement; and had little or nothing to offer us now except skins.

'They are nominal Christians: their marriages are performed without any ceremony: and all the elders sit in council to manage their affairs; all the young, from ten up to a certain age, are considered a standing militia, and are armed with long pikes; they have no books or paper, nor any schools; they retain a certain observance of the sabbath by refraining from their daily labours, and perform a short superstitious ceremony on that day all together; and they may be considered almost a new race of beings.'

It would have been easy to dismiss this report straight away, but then Peter produced another item. This was an English translation, reproduced below, of a passage from *Tijdschrift voor Nederlandsch Indie* (vol. 13, no. 12, p. 361), a Dutch scientific magazine published in 1851:

In 1836 an English merchant ship arrived in Samarang where I was the harbour master. The captain, whose name I have forgotten, told me that he had just come from the north coast of New Holland and that some of the passengers on board his ship who had travelled into the interior had met [there] about 300 Hollanders living in a totally primitive manner.

I reported to the Governor-General De Eerens what the captain had related to me, but have never heard anything more about the matter. I did read a story of this kind later in an English newspaper. Probably this story is the basis for the account in Nederlandsch Magazyn *of 1837 p. 179, which relates that some English travellers in the Raffles Bay area, on the west coast of New Holland, had encountered about 300 Hollanders in the interior; they were dressed in hides and their chief was descended from an officer named Van Bearle. They related to the travellers that their ancestors had been shipwrecked some 170 years ago; 10 women had also survived the wreck. They lived in a very backward civilisation. Sundays were still honoured when they refrained from work.*

The article was signed by a chap called van Bloomestein, who had gotten his dates mixed up a little, but to me that was unimportant. What mattered was that here was a confirmation of Nixon's account.

Peter had put all the time he could spare into trying to authenticate these claims but had basically drawn a blank. He threw the problem over to me to see if I could come up with some sort of result. At the time I didn't take the articles too seriously. Nixon's story sounded like an eighteenth century traveller's tale that had been spread around, but it was an interesting yarn, so I took it home, put it in the bottom drawer and didn't think much more about it.

Some months later I was fossicking around in that bottom drawer and there was the *Leeds Mercury* article. I picked it up and read it again, really carefully this time. Paying a bit more attention to the style of writing, I noticed a number of interesting points about the story that made me think that perhaps it might be authentic.

Initially, the most striking point was that traditionally, people who claim to have found lost tribes or civilisations describe them in glowing terms—the sort of Rider H Haggard stuff that was very popular back in those days. Yet this was no 'El Dorado', no utopian description: the Dutch were eking out a scant existence in a harsh environment. There was nothing romantic about it at all.

Not only that, but I also detected a rather interesting change of attitude towards the Dutch colony in Nixon's report. Initially he was flushed with excitement and expectation at what he saw: . . . *no words can express the astonishment, delight and wonder*

The Tanami Desert is a huge flat plain covered with spinifex, shrubs, trees and termite mounds.

I felt at the magical change of scenery . . . It seemed as if enchantment had brought me to a civilised country . . . but after spending eight days living in the settlement his attitude changed noticeably: . . . *they have no animals of the domestic kind . . . their plantations consist only of maize and yams . . . they frequently experience a scarcity and shortage of provisions most probably owing to ignorance and mismanagement.* His final comment is almost dismissive in its tone: . . . *they retain a certain observance of the Sabbath by refraining from their daily labours and perform a short superstitious ceremony on that day all together; and they may be considered a new race of beings.*

This 'before' and 'after' comparison of Nixon's words suggests a degree of dissatisfaction with the situation after spending eight days living in the Dutch colony.

To me it also started to reinforce the likely authenticity of the report.

Looking at the numbers used by the Dutch, I noticed they were all multiples of ten: ten sisters, 80 males, children over the age of ten and so forth. This rounding off process could be very much expected in the circumstances, with no writing material available and only a hand-me-down source of mathematical skill.

At this point I thought I'd better get out a map and plot Nixon's latitude and longitude for the Dutch colony's location. This turned out to be in the northern sector of the Tanami Desert—not a very good start. You'd think that the waterway described

in the narrative would be shown on the map, but of course it wasn't.

Now you've got to remember that at the time of the Nixon expedition (1832), latitude and longitude had a tendency to be slightly incorrect, depending on the skills of the operator and the precision of his watch or chronometer. Latitude was generally fairly accurate, but longitude could be quite wonky. As a result I initially assumed the latitude to be correct.

Then in the middle of the night I woke up wondering where Nixon's longitude would fit if I took it further to the north. I went back to the map and extended the line of longitude 800 kilometres to the north of the fix Nixon had given for the Dutch colony. Not only did it cut through Raffles Bay—it intersected almost exactly the location of the old British establishment, Fort Wellington, which had most probably been Nixon's landing and starting off point for the expedition. Although the Fort had been abandoned two years before Nixon's arrival, the remains of huts and water wells were still there, and no doubt Nixon and his men would have made use of them.

This line of longitude raises a few interesting points. It was just too much of a coincidence that his longitude line for Mount Singapore also ran all the way north and cut right through his starting point. Nixon was clearly aware of the position of Fort Wellington within Raffles Bay, and most likely it represented the first and last accurate longitudinal reading throughout the entire two months of the expedition. I'd reckon that the ship's chronometer was probably much more accurate than anything he carried himself in the field.

In 1832 the coastline to the south of Fort Wellington had already been charted by both Matthew Flinders and Captain Phillip Parker King. It's quite likely that personnel previously based at Fort Wellington would have explored some of the land mass to the south-east, perhaps giving Nixon an idea of the task that lay ahead of him. You see, before travelling due south from the Fort, it would have been necessary to skirt around Van Diemen Gulf. From there, the Arnhem Land escarpment would have edged Nixon and his men round to the east a little. Then they could have followed a compass bearing; when it was time to return, it would have been a simple process to reverse direction, head north, and find a way back around the Arnhem Land escarpment and Van Diemen Gulf to their starting point at Fort Wellington.

It struck me that this is a quick, efficient way to navigate in a short space of time. You'd never feel lost because you'd just head in one direction, along one basic compass bearing—south. I now felt inspired enough to really pull the article to bits.

Back in 1832, very few people had heard of Raffles Bay, yet Nixon also referred to it by its alternative name, Port Raffles. Only someone with local knowledge would have been familiar with both of those names. The geographical descriptions are also very accurate, yet no one had explored the northern Australian landmass at that time. Use of words such as kangaroo, cockatoo, tribe and Aborigines also suggests at least some exposure to the Australian environment.

Nixon's description of the watercourse running east-west is quite accurate when you look at water catchments in sand dune country in the wet season. The sand dunes quite often produce parallel rows of vegetation as described, and the distance of half a mile between dunes is about right, so perhaps he was looking at water trapped between parallel sand dunes. The waterway described was quite possibly the result of a big wet season rather than a permanent fixture, and the 'islands' could have been formed by vegetation protruding through seasonal floodwaters at that time of year. Further, the surrounding countryside is portrayed as 'low and level', which perfectly describes the countryside at the given latitude and longitude.

If the report were a work of fiction, why provide an accurate location fix at all? The announcement of such a find would undoubtedly encourage further possible expeditions into the location. Surely it would be better to say that no accurate reading had been taken, or to make up some sort of excuse. But he didn't do that, which was beginning to make me think that the report was real—scary stuff.

In 1832, the popular opinion was that the centre of Australia was a vast inland sea. Yet Nixon's report contradicts that dream and in fact confirms the geographical reality. Because his account was not widely published or taken seriously at the time, the debate about the centre of the Australian continent raged on for many more years.

According to Nixon's time frame, it took his party 35 days to travel nearly 800 kilometres inland. That would allow them an average of 23 kilometres travel per day. Now John McDouall Stuart covered a distance of 2414 kilometres in three months, which averages out at 27.3 kilometres a day. On many occasions, Stuart managed to travel over 48 kilometres in one day even when there was no water for his horses. And once, in the same desert country that Nixon would have crossed, Stuart noted the day's travel at 40 miles (64 kilometres), so Nixon's time and space didn't concern me.

Finally I asked myself, if such a 'great wall' existed, why hadn't it been discovered since Nixon's 1832 visit? As it happens, very few people have examined or even visited the countryside in question. No explorers, anthropologists, graziers or tourists—in fact you could count on one hand the number of people who have been through that general area. There's no overhead air traffic, no cattle industry, not even information

The Kimberley coast. Many Dutch ships came to grief on the west coast of Australia on their way to Batavia.

on any tribal Aboriginal group occupying that country. Even to this day, Nixon could not have picked a more remote and unexplored area if he'd tried.

By the time I'd figured all of this out, I was well and truly hooked on the mystery. It's an established fact that unknown numbers of Dutch ships have foundered on the west coast of Australia. There was a really good reason for this. During the seventeenth and eighteenth centuries, when trade between Holland and the East Indies was at its peak, common sailing practice was to round the Cape of Good Hope at the bottom of Africa, then head due east towards 'the great south land', as Australia was known, before changing course to the north for Batavia, the headquarters of the Dutch East India Company (or VOC, as it was called).

You really had to have your wits about you sailing in those days, because the waters off the west coast of Australia can be treacherous, and reefs and islands crop up unexpectedly. No one knows exactly how many ships were wrecked, nor how many crew and passengers survived and made it to the western shores of Australia. Over the years, however, evidence has been found that suggests that some survivors lived with local Australian Aboriginal people along the western coastline.

Over the last 20 years I've crossed the Tanami Desert too many times to remember and believe me, you should be well prepared. Tanami landscape is peppered with spinifex, turpentine bushes and termite mounds, and there's precious little reliable water.

When I first plotted on a map
Nixon's latitude and longitude
for the Dutch colony's location,
it turned out to be in the
northern sector of the Tanami
Desert—not a very good start.

Even today the Kimberley is considered one of the most isolated parts of Australia. When Smithy and his crew passed over this area in 1929 they were flying blind, so missed seeing perfect navigational landmarks such as Mount Casuarina and the Berkley River, pictured here.

Rugged, towering rocky cliffs line a number of rivers that flow through the Kimberley and dump directly into the Indian Ocean.

My next line of thought was that if there had been a large group of Dutch people living in inland Australia for over 100 years, there should be some Aboriginal information or knowledge to support that fact. The first European explorer to record information about Aboriginal people in the Tanami area was John McDouall Stuart, and in his journals a number of anecdotes indicate that the Warramunga he encountered may have been influenced by contact with outside sources. As I've recounted these stories in the previous chapter, there's no need to go over them again.

Tribal maps show that the Binjonjgona once inhabited the area in which Nixon claimed to have found the Dutch settlement, but almost nothing has been recorded in the literature about these people, and in the last 100 years they have completely disappeared. However, the surrounding tribal groups, such as the Warramunga, the Walpiri and the Gurinji, are very well known in anthropological circles.

But why were the Warramunga so influenced and not other tribal groups that we know of? Remember this Dutch settlement wasn't a hunter-gatherer one. It was basically sustained by cultivated crops, supplemented by local natural resources. There was no need to roam the countryside to find food as the Aborigines did. For the Dutch, foraging would have been limited because they had a permanent base.

A handful of honey ants, like these in the Tanami Desert, make a sweet, tasty snack that gives you a small burst of energy. You have to dig in the ground to find them, but it's worthwhile.

According to Nixon's latitude and longitude the Dutch settlement was much closer to the tribal area of the Warramunga than to that of any other Aboriginal group. The Gurindji, for instance, were much further to the west of the Dutch than the Warramunga were to the east of them, and the Mudbara and Djingili were even further to the north and north-east respectively. Geographically it was simply a matter of distance that forced the Dutch to have more association with the Warramunga. Access to resources may have been another reason, and perhaps the Warramunga were more open to such an association.

There's one other factor to consider. In the area of the Dutch settlement, the dominating sand dunes naturally channel travellers in an east-south-easterly direction. Sixty-five kilometres of travel would have brought them slap bang into the Warramunga tribal area.

The first people to record Warramunga history seriously were the anthropologists Baldwin Spencer and Frank Gillen at the turn of the century. Although the work of these two pioneer anthropologists has been heavily criticised by some of the academic fraternity in recent years, it was important for me to go to the people who had recorded the first contact information. Without doubt those people were Spencer and Gillen; despite the criticism, the work they conducted back in 1899 and 1901 stands alone.

There was some very encouraging detail in Spencer and Gillen's research notes. For instance, here we have a group of Aborigines living in Central Australia who, in one of their ancestral myths, describe a particular group of women who travel across the countryside and were supposed to have come from a country beyond the sea. Now why on earth are Aboriginal people in Central Australia talking about a group of women who came from a country beyond the sea? It just doesn't fit.

Other myths and legends of the Warramunga support the theory of possible early European contact, such as the story of an ancestral being who used to hang flesh he couldn't eat up in trees to keep till he wanted it. Now that action sounds to me like wind or sun drying, which was never an Aboriginal practice as far as I'm aware. Remember, verbal storylines are often not very old. That is to say, the elements they cover may be only a few generations old and may span just a couple of hundred years.

In the collection of photographs taken by Spencer and Gillen I was struck by images showing elders whose facial hairs had been plucked away from the side of the face and the top lip. It was a basic form of shaving, I guess. The resulting appearance makes them look a lot like aristocratic northern European men of a few centuries ago.

Something that's always fascinated me on my travels through Central Australia is the appearance of blonde-haired Aboriginal people, particularly children. Now if this Dutch story of Nixon's is true, then perhaps we have the start of an explanation.

Spencer and Gillen go on to offer further evidence that could lend credit to the theory:

The men of the Warramunga Tribe especially strike one as having a good physique. This is rather difficult to account for, as their country does not appear to be so good, from the point of view of food supply, as that of the Arunta, more especially those living in the large area occupied by the McDonnald Ranges, where there is rarely any lack of food or water.

Linguistics is not a subject that I pretend to understand anything about, but an eminent linguist by the name of Capell has analysed elements of the Warramunga language and made the following remark.

> *The student of Australian language cannot but be struck by the wide departure from the common Australian roots . . . It is in this arrangement that the Warramunga differs so markedly from the other languages of the Northern Territory.*

This brings me to another interesting point. Grahame Walsh's book, *Australia's Greatest Rock Art*, has an impressive collection of some of the most striking rock art known to exist in Australia. A number of art sites that lie along a possible track or trail from the Dutch colony location to the West Australian coastline could arguably be termed 'of doubtful origin'. The most obvious of these are certain engravings or petroglyphs, which Aboriginal people themselves deny as being part of their culture.

A classic example is the rock engraving located at a spring near Stuart Creek station, not far from the border of Western Australia and the Northern Territory. Known as the 'Knight in Armour', the engraving was discovered many years ago by a member of a geological expedition. Dr Ian Crawford, in his book, *Art of the Wandjina*, makes the following comment:

> *The style of the engraving does not look Aboriginal, and the technique by which the figure is formed by a series of round pits is unlike any I have seen.*

A number of strange rock engravings or petroglyphs, which Aborigines say are not part of their culture, may be a clue to the existence of the Dutch settlement.

One aspect that struck me about the story of the Dutch colony was the vast distance they had to travel across arid country like this when they moved from the west coast to inland Australia. These days it would be pretty hard to traverse so much waterless country, but as it turns out the weather patterns were quite different back then.

Another thing that struck me was the fact that the shipwrecked survivors had travelled all the way from the west coast to the interior of Australia before settling down. These days it would be pretty hard to get across so much waterless country, but I wondered if perhaps the weather patterns were at all different back then.

This line of research led me to recent scientific studies of coral conducted by scientists at the Australian Institute of Marine Science (AIMS). You see, when corals are growing they incorporate into their skeletons molecules absorbed from the surrounding waters. By drilling cores from the corals and examining their structure it's possible to determine how much rain has fallen at any given stage of the coral's life, which can be up to 1000 years.

The fresh water flushing out of the river systems carries decayed vegetation products, which the coral incorporates as annual fluorescent bands as it grows. So you can tell which years had big wet seasons and which had small ones, and this is exactly what Dr Peter Isdale at AIMS has done. So far he has wound the clock back to the year 1600, which isn't bad. The resulting information reveals that some wet seasons during the 1600s and 1700s were much bigger than any we've experienced since. This in turn would suggest that during these big seasons it would have been possible to follow the river systems and waterways from the coast inland.

But that's not all. In a 1950 book titled *I Saw a Strange Land*, Arthur Groom relates the reply given by a Central Australian Aborigine to a question on the origin of various feral animals:

Rabbita—he only come to this country little while. Pappy-dawg—wild dog—been here alla time. Horse and cattle come before rabbita. Pussy-cat he come long, long time ago—before sheepee an' bullocky an' camella. My people tell me—pussy-cat come that way' he nodded to the west. 'Long time ago—before white people come, big boat come that way and pussy-cat jump off, run about find 'nother pussy-cat, and now big mob pussy-cat everywhere, run about desert country alla' time; eat little birds—lizards—eat close up everything.'

As luck would have it, Paul Wagner, a Macquarie University PhD student, is writing a thesis on the origin of cats in Australia. He is focusing on collecting genetic material from feral cats from different parts of Australia, and seeing if it matches with that of cats from possible source populations in Holland, Portugal, Indonesia or England.

The Dutch settled New York city and South Africa at about the same time as they were getting shipwrecked off the West Australian coast. As minimal genetic changes have occurred in cats of Dutch origin in both South Africa and New York, it's possible to compare their genetic make-up with that of feral cats in Australia.

Paul hasn't finished his research yet, but the evidence so far points to the arrival of cats up to 300 years before European settlement in Central Australia. He mentioned that apart from the genetic evidence, there was the Aboriginal testimony, plus the sudden extinction of lots of small mammals.

But let's return to the original article. The real questions are: who was this Lieutenant Nixon, where did he come from and why was his expedition shrouded in secrecy? Digging through the Mitchell Library archives in Sydney, I made some very interesting discoveries.

In the early days of British settlement in Singapore the Honourable East India Company (HEC) ran the show. This was a private enterprise company with shareholders

Reptiles like this skink are well adapted to life in the Tanami Desert. Camouflage helps protect them from predators, and it takes a really keen eye to distinguish them from their background.

and directors based in London, although the immediate bosses of the Singapore mob were based much closer, in India. Because of the problems of distance and communication, the Singapore branch of the company operated somewhat independently. Before long, intense rivalry developed between the British and the Dutch, who were operating in the nearby East Indies.

As a result, units from the Indian Army were sent to Singapore to provide security. The HEC was virtually a law unto itself. As an example, in the 1800s they decided to invade Java to take over from the Dutch without even informing Britain. The first thing the English Parliament knew about this incident was when the HEC announced that they had seized the island from the Dutch.

The odds are, given that Lieutenant Nixon and his men came to Australia from Singapore, they were most likely to have been based there with the Indian Army. Now it turns out that records of the Indian Army and the HEC are held in the India Office Collection of the British Library in London.

Enter Karen and Andrew Cook, a husband and wife team, both doctors of philosophy, who work at the British Library. Since I first contacted them they've been heavily involved in researching the Nixon story, and it's their work that has uncovered a lot of this information.

Early on in the piece, before we tried to pin down our Lieutenant Nixon, Karen Cook discovered the likely identity of the 'nameless correspondent living near Halifax' who had originally sent Nixon's story to the *Leeds Mercury*. We believe him to be one Lieutenant Maslen, a retired officer of the Honourable East India Company's Service.

Back in 1830, Maslen published a book titled *The Friend of Australia; or, a plan for exploring the interior, and for carrying on a survey of the whole continent of Australia.* This book was written by Maslen at his home, just near a village called Blackstone Edge. A quick look at a map of England shows that Blackstone Edge is just a few miles outside Halifax.

The book spells out how to explore Australia, based on Maslen's experiences in remote parts of India. It includes maps and illustrations and is absolutely fascinating. Maslen argues long and hard that internal exploration of Australia should be an immediate priority for the British Government, with particular emphasis on Central

Australia. One suggestion he offers was to start from Raffles Bay, using HEC resources. The expedition would establish a base camp, where some men would remain. The rest would move about 160 kilometres south to set up a depot, again leaving some men. The men left in camp would make mini-expeditions to the east and west to see what they could learn. Meanwhile the rest would move another 160 kilometres south, establish another depot and so on.

In the last four years I've made five expeditions, covering thousands of square kilometres, to search for the site of the old Dutch settlement. It's a long process of elimination and it's not over yet.

Maslen gives details of all the requirements for such an expedition, including numbers of men, bullocks, stores and equipment. It's an extraordinary book, and it's quite likely that Nixon had seen a copy of it before he departed on his expedition. In fact the book could have provided the inspiration for Nixon's expedition in the first place.

As to Nixon himself, Andrew Cook's initial research into the archival records revealed that the only army units listed in Singapore in 1832 were Madras units. Further research showed that there were four Lt Nixons in the Madras Army at that time. Of these, the current most likely candidate is a Lt John William Nixon, born 3 February 1809, educated at Mr James Brown's Academy, Madras. The trouble with him, however, is that he was based in Singapore in 1827 and 1828, not 1832. His service record shows a gap between June 1828 and May 1833, so we don't really know what he was doing at that time. So far, he's our best Nixon candidate. He died in India in 1839, aged just 30 years.

Nixon aside, his exploring party was most likely made up of Indian soldiers of the Madras Native Infantry, who could have handled the trying conditions of the expedition much better than the average English soldier at the time. Eventually all of these men would have returned to India, where no one has heard from them since.

But why the original need for secrecy? That question takes us back again to the HEC's style of operation in Singapore. By 1830 the company had become a giant bureaucracy and was going broke. Consequently the Governor of Singapore was recalled and not replaced for some years. The public service was cut in half and employees' salaries reduced by two-thirds. The locals were not happy, discontent was rife, and some of the residents decided to get involved in private enterprise. The bosses back in India got to hear of these activities and weren't impressed. In fact they issued an order strictly forbidding HEC employees from undertaking such activities.

Meanwhile, Fort Wellington, the British establishment at Raffles Bay, set up at the request of the HEC's Trade Committee, helped to consolidate their position in the Dutch archipelago region, and could possibly have served as a second trading base in northern Australia. But within two years the British Government backed out, and it took the HEC another eight years of intense lobbying before the government had another go, this time establishing a settlement at Port Essington.

I might add that when the British Government closed down Raffles Bay in 1829 after only two years of operation, the HEC people in Singapore thought it was an absolute disgrace and were appalled that so little effort had been put into the small outpost by the British Government. It helps to remember here that the British Government and the HEC were two separate organisations, and they quite often opposed each other.

By the early 1830s, the time was ripe for a Singapore-based private enterprise group to organise an expedition to explore northern Australia, keeping the undertaking secret. In all probability neither the bosses in India nor the government of New South Wales would have been in the know.

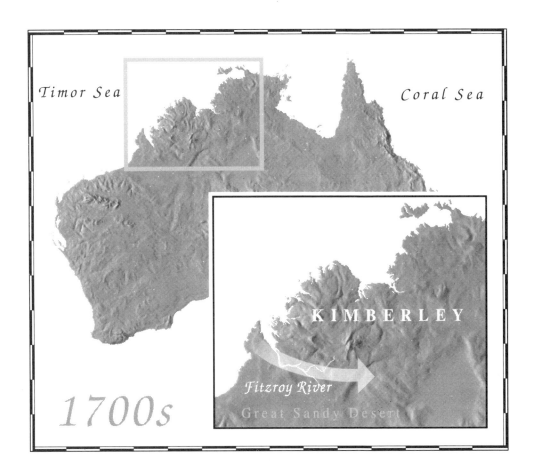

The tenuous political situation between the HEC and the British Parliament begins to explain, at least in part, the reason for the Company's reluctance to broadcast widely their expedition in New Holland with Nixon. Of course, had Nixon discovered something of commercial wealth (such as coal or, better still, gold) then things may have been different. I imagine that in those days of colonial expansion, the HEC would have preferred to keep to itself news of the discovery of a Dutch settlement in Central Australia.

This would also help to explain why no traces of Nixon's expedition have been found—or have they? I've always been intrigued by the explorer Gregory's description of a camp-site he found in July 1856, at the junction of Elsey and Birdum Creeks, not far from Mataranka in the Northern Territory. Gregory believed the camp to have been made by Ludwig Leichhardt because, as Gregory put it, Leichhardt was the only person in the field at the time (the only person Gregory knew of, more likely).

Gregory's claim has never rung true to me for a number of reasons. First, the site is way north of Leichhardt's intended route between Moreton Bay on the east coast and the Swan River settlement on the west. Secondly, no other camp-sites have been found in that vicinity. And thirdly, the amount of charcoal found at the camp-site made Gregory believe that it had been occupied for several weeks, and by a large number of people. This is more in keeping with what we know of Nixon's set-up than Leichhardt's. Gregory conducted a thorough search of the area, hoping to find a blazed tree or some other sign that might indicate just who had camped there. He found nothing, which is most unlike Leichhardt, who always blazed trees in his camp-sites.

To Gregory's knowledge, Leichhardt (who disappeared in 1848) was the only other explorer who could have passed through that region before his own North Australian Exploring Expedition of 1856. But the unknown camp is pretty well on the line of longitude that extends south towards Central Australia from Raffles Bay. I suspect that the camp-site found by Gregory was one of Nixon's depot camps, established on his march due south from Raffles Bay.

A recent discovery of two skeletons in the Simpson Desert suggests it's likely that Leichhardt did not travel to the north from the Roma area where he was last seen. Instead he may have tried to continue in a more or less direct line west, and perished in the harsh semi-arid zone of northern South Australia.

During the couple of years that I've spent researching the Nixon story, I've had the opportunity to get out and look for the site of the Dutch settlement, both on the ground and from the air. To fit the narration given by Nixon, the location involved must have the following elements:

- A long watercourse nearly in a straight line east to west. As Nixon may well have been describing the residue from the 1831–32 wet season, it needn't be a flat sheet of water, and in fact may not always be so obvious.
- A hill or low mountain, complete with rock, five or six kilometres to the north.
- Permanent water throughout the year, sufficient for 200+ people.
- Possibly palm trees to the south of the watercourse.
- Rock or sandstone in the general area from which a so-called 'great wall' could have been made.
- Water catchments of sufficient size to supply fish.

- An area closely associated with the course of a rivulet.

- The hill (Nixon's Mount Singapore) must be positioned in such a way that from it you could observe the waterway disappearing to the west as far as the eye could see, and yet be able to discern that the waterway appears to sweep to the south at its eastern end. Therefore the hill must be closer to the eastern end than the western end of the waterway.

It's over 160 years since Lieutenant Nixon walked away from the Dutch settlement. Much has changed in that relatively short space of time, even rainfall and vegetation patterns. As we continue our research, my colleagues and I are finding out more and more information all the time. This ongoing project is really exciting, and the outcome is looking positive. I guess not a week goes by without another piece of the jigsaw puzzle fitting into place, either here in Australia, over in England or, more recently, in Holland and Indonesia.

In the last four years I've made five expeditions to search for Nixon's location. Some of these have been quick helicopter trips, but I reckon all up I would have spent months and months on the job, covering thousands of square kilometres. It's a long process of elimination, and that's the way I've been attacking it—eliminating one possible site after another. But one of the great things about Australia is that it's big enough to contain intriguing mysteries like this. I suspect that this story is not yet over, and Australia in the near future will give up one of its long-held secrets.

On 31 March, 1929, over a
hundred thousand people waved
Smithy and his mates off when
they departed from Richmond
Airport, New South Wales on
the first leg of their flight to
London in the Southern Cross.

CHAPTER SEVEN

COFFEE ROYAL AND THE *KOOKABURRA*

IF YOU STOP for a moment to think about modern-day communication systems, the mind fairly boggles. Picture this: I'm sitting alone in my Land Rover on a bush track in the Kimberley 10 or 12 hours' drive from Derby, the nearest town. I need to check up and confirm a helicopter booking I've made for next week—what do I do? Simply reach over to the satellite mobile phone, dial up the number and Bob's your uncle.

It hasn't always been this easy. Over 60 years ago two very well-known Australians got themselves into a lot of strife because of poor communications. And it all began with a piece of aerial wire.

Let's wind back a bit to

the late 1920s, when Charles Kingsford Smith and Charles Ulm were national heroes. In the famous *Southern Cross* they'd established flying records across the Pacific, the Tasman and the Australian continent. Then, on 12 December 1928, they set up Australian National Airways with the aim of providing scheduled services to major Australian locations—the first airline using multi-engined aircraft to do so.

Smithy and Ulm employed the best air and ground crews and set aside enough capital to buy five of the latest Avro '618–ten' aircraft. These were to be built under licence in England by AV Roe & Co.

Next year, company business required a visit

to Manchester in England to take delivery of the aircraft and to hire pilots and engineers for the airline. The two partners decided to fly there. With Tom McWilliams on board as radio operator and Harold Litchfield ('Litch' as he was known to his mates) as navigator, Smithy and Ulm left Sydney in the *Southern Cross* on 31 March 1929, in good weather. Over a hundred thousand people waved them off at Richmond Airport; Smithy was everybody's hero, and this was a grand occasion.

Funnily enough the *Southern Cross* has outlasted the pilots, and you can see it to this day, restored to its former glory and enshrined in a special memorial on the way out to Brisbane Airport. The *Southern Cross*, call-sign VHS-USU, is a Fokker F VII b-3m monoplane powered by three Wright Whirlwind J5 200 hp engines. One engine is attached to the front of the fuselage, the others suspended under the wing in nacelles. In normal flying conditions each engine would have used 45 to 55 litres an hour.

The *Southern Cross* is made of timber. It's 22 metres long, with a wingspan about the same. The fuselage is a tubular, welded structure covered in weatherproof fabric. Two main spars of laminated spruce with an outer covering of plywood provide support. The undercarriage has a rubber suspension with two wire-spoked wheels mounted on plain bearings. There's one tail-skid, but no brakes. Four 320-litre tanks are installed in the wing, directly over the fuselage. The cockpit is sort of half-enclosed for a crew of two sitting side-by-side.

When I say half-enclosed, I mean the side windows left a bit to be desired, because basically there weren't any, and when the rain came from the side you had to just sit there and cop it. Those back in the passenger cabin were much better off.

In 1929, when Smithy and his mates were preparing to leave for England, the *Southern Cross* was looking a little the worse for wear. The outer fabric was worn and faded and the metal surfaces had lost their sheen. But the 'Old Bus', as she was affectionately known, was definitely airworthy.

About half an hour after take-off, Litch apparently opened one of the sliding glass windows in the cabin so he could lean out and get a sighting of the sun. He was the navigator, and these were early days of the aviation industry, so some of the instruments were a bit primitive by today's standards. To find out roughly where they were, the navigator would take a reading from the sun, or at night the stars, using a sextant. That way they would come up with a latitude. By combining that latitude reading with the compass direction and the speed of the aircraft, they could get a reasonable fix on their position. Mind you, the maps they were using in those days weren't all that flash, but they didn't have much choice.

Anyway, as Litch was taking his bearing out the window, he accidentally knocked the locking mechanism on the long wave aerial's drum, causing it to unroll and fall away from the plane. At this point it might be a good idea to explain how communications systems worked on aircraft in those days. They had two separate systems, one for transmitting messages and one for receiving. Each system had its own aerial; the transmitter's was fixed to the top of the plane and the receiver's wound out from a drum, with a small weight attached, trailing below and behind the plane. You see, this aerial was a bit like a long wire rolled up on a fishing reel, and when it was unlocked, it just ran itself right out until there was nothing left—no more wire, no more line.

Sounds like a disaster, but what it meant was that the men could now only transmit messages and not receive them. We could stop and learn something here, I suppose: don't forget to secure one end of your floating aerial to your drum before you take-off! In other words, if you're setting off on an adventure, thoroughly check your gear before you leave home.

When he discovered what had happened, Litch told McWilliams, who passed a note to Smithy suggesting they turn back to Sydney to fit a new aerial. But Smithy realised that in order to land safely they'd have to dump over 3000 litres of fuel. Besides that, the weather looked good, so he decided to fly on to Wyndham, their first scheduled stop.

At about that same time, the Richmond airport radio operator was trying to contact the *Southern Cross*. He'd received a telegraphed message from Wyndham that the flight should not depart from Sydney as the weather conditions had seriously deteriorated. The four men continued on in quiet ignorance of all this till just north of Alice Springs, when they found themselves flying into blinding red dust, whipped up by the fierce electrical storms that now confronted them. With visibility reduced to zero they had to rely on dead reckoning by compass to find their way to Wyndham.

In his book, *My Flying Life*, Smithy described the conditions:

the weather became worse. Torrential rain poured down, and hour after hour I flew on blind . . .

Litchfield, of course, could get no sights in the blinding rain and dense cloud that surrounded us. It was a horrible night, and we looked eagerly forward to the morning and to our arrival at Wyndham, where we were due at 10.30 Wyndham time, which is one and a half hours behind Sydney time.

Smithy had originally planned to refuel at Wyndham, but now they were lost.

The Kimberley region over which the men were flying is one of my favourite parts of Australia. It's in the north-west corner, bounded by the Timor Sea to the north, the Indian Ocean to the west and the Great Sandy Desert to the south. The West Australian–Northern Territory border marks the eastern end of the region. The Kimberley covers about 345 250 square kilometres, and in case that doesn't mean much to you, the whole of the United Kingdom is only 244 000 square kilometres.

Even today the Kimberley is considered one the most isolated parts of Australia. That's probably because it's the furthest away from our major east coast cities. The early pioneers started arriving there in the 1880s, some droving cattle from the east and others chasing gold—not to forget the missionaries who hoped to save the souls of the local Aboriginal people. The place still has a frontier feel about it—exciting too, I can tell you. The landscape is absolutely spectacular; its most noticeable features are jumbled red rocky outcrops, boab trees and spiky spinifex grass. Its a harsh environment, and it can jump up and grab you if you don't know what you're doing.

As the cloud cover began breaking up after dawn, the men caught glimpses of the land below. Smithy reckoned he'd *never seen such an inhospitable terrain of ravines, roaring torrents, cliffs, heavy timber, and an entire absence of any habitation.* When they got to the coast they were greeted by wild seas and no sign of Wyndham. After an hour of fruitless searching, Smithy decided to follow the coast in a north-westerly direction, figuring that they'd overshot the mark. As they still had enough fuel, this was a better option than trying to cut overland with the risk of losing their way in

The Kimberley, one of my favourite parts of Australia, covers more than 345,000 square kilometres. It's bounded by the Timor Sea to the north, the Indian Ocean to the west and the Great Sandy Desert to the south. The West Australia/ Northern Territory border marks its eastern extremity.

There's a good variety of bush tucker in mangrove country if you know what to look for. You'd search these mangrove prop roots looking for the mangrove snails (Nerita sp.) that crawl up them at high tide.

Kimberley country—wild and spectacular. Pictured are tidal 'horizontal waterfalls' which rush in and out of Kimberley inlets.

If, like Lasseter, you're going to spend time in Central Australia's salt lake environment, you should really bone up on it first. The middle of lakes like these are generally a quagmire—don't even think about walking or driving across the top.

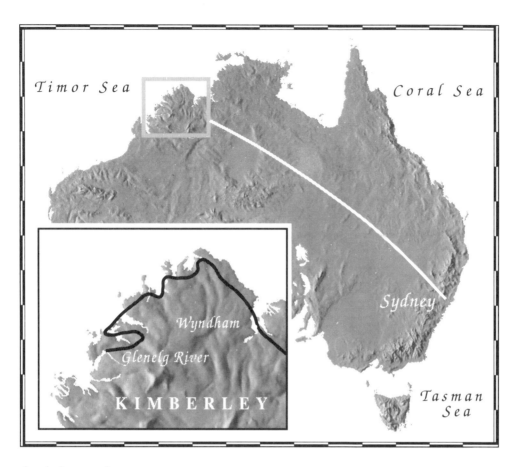

the dodgy weather.

A couple of hours later there was still no sign of Wyndham, but they did spot a couple of European huts—Drysdale Mission as a matter of fact. Ulm dropped a weight with a message attached, *Please indicate direction of Wyndham*, out the open window. Unfortunately the note wasn't found, but seeing a plane circling overhead (obviously a sign of some kind of problem) the helpful locals pointed towards the closest available landing place, which happened to be in a south-westerly direction. Another breakdown in communication.

Until then Smithy and Ulm had been convinced that Wyndham lay to the south-east, but accepting that the locals must know the area better, they turned the plane towards the south-west, flying in appalling weather for what seemed like forever. They were now desperately low on fuel and well and truly lost.

With just a few hours' of petrol left they spotted another group of huts (Port George Mission, as they later found out). As they circled above it, Ulm dropped another note which read, *Please place white sheets pointing direction of Wyndham, and mark in large figures number of miles.* This time the message was picked up, and shortly afterwards they were horrified to see the figures 250 marked on a plain white strip pointing to the east.

Smithy spun the plane round and flew east for almost an hour. He then realised that, *the only resource left was to crash as gracefully as possible in that terrible country.* I rather like those words, 'crash as gracefully as possible'—I suppose if you have to crash-land, a graceful crash is the way to do it! The idea they had was to fly back and land as close as they could to the mission they'd just passed so that help would be close at hand. But visibility was limited because of the continuing bad weather and they couldn't find the mission again. Smithy had to get down on the deck—and quickly. Luckily he caught sight of a mudflat and landed on it at 80 kilometres an hour, the wheels sinking into the mud. The plane lurched and tilted dangerously, but Smithy skilfully managed to pull it up about a metre short of a tree.

Estuaries along the Kimberley coast are alive with saltwater crocodiles. Together with boggy ground and mangrove swamps, they didn't enhance the situation in which Smithy, Ulm, Litch and McWilliams found themselves after their forced landing in 1929.

Meanwhile McWilliams had been sending out precise details of their predicament. His radio messages had been picked up all over Australia, so the whole country knew what was going on—that was, until they landed the plane. The last message McWilliams was able to transmit said, *We are about to make a forced landing in bad country.*

In fact Smithy had landed the *Southern Cross* on the Glenelg River tidal flats on the Kimberley coast, about 220 kilometres to the west of Wyndham. It was the tail end of the wet season. Luckily no one was hurt and the plane was okay, except that it was out of fuel, and in any case the ground was too wet to take off. The wheels had sunk right into the mud to such a point that it was basically bogged.

Just try to imagine how they must have felt as they got out of the plane and took a look around. After 28 hours in the air they were deaf from the noise of the engines, tired and hungry. It was late afternoon and they had no idea where they were, or how they could get out. Remember, back in those days there were no good maps for aviators. All these blokes had with them were some Admiralty charts, two general maps of Australia and the Times Atlas.

And as for tucker—well, that was a pretty sad story.

We spent a bad night, plagued by mosquitoes and depressed by the discovery that the emergency rations which ought to have been in a locker were unaccountably missing. We never discovered what had happened to them, and can only conclude that they had been stolen before we started by someone who was either hungry or wanted a souvenir.

This is what the four men had to live on: a couple of sandwiches left over from the previous day, a flask of coffee, and another of brandy. As luck would have it they'd been asked to take along 10 pounds of Allenbury's baby food for a sick baby in Wyndham.

Next morning the sun came out, and apart from being annoyed by the flies, the men felt much more positive. They mixed some baby food with water to make a kind of gruel or porridge and brewed up a bit of weak coffee, laced with about a quarter of the brandy—'Coffee Royal', Smithy called it, not realising that those words would return to haunt him time and time again.

With the sun bright and clear in the sky, Litch was able to take morning and afternoon sightings and calculate their position. When they checked their chart they discovered that no kind of habitation lay in the area. According to Smithy,

We held a council of war, and decided that we must keep a good smoke fire burning, to attract attention; that we must rig up the short-wave aerial so that McWilliams could listen in, and that a search for some kind of food was imperative.

What the men proposed was to make a fire that would create lots of smoke, and they decided to build their fire on top of a hill. On the Glenelg River tidal flats, that's easier said than done. For starters, at that time of the year (the tail end of the wet season) there'd be very little dry wood. Besides that, the men would have to spend a lot of time and energy trudging up and down a hill to feed their fire. And then there was the added problem of trying to produce thick smoke.

Some armchair critics later suggested that the crew should have burnt engine oil or one of the rubber tyres to create smoke. The trouble is, this kind of smoke is black, and because the landscape looks dark from the air the smoke blends in pretty quickly. Smithy reckoned that white smoke would be more obvious, so they fed the fire with damp grass. White smoke is certainly more noticeable than black smoke, but I wouldn't want to stake my life on it, especially on a windy day. (Now here's a handy survival hint: the best way to attract attention during the day is to use a signal mirror. It's light, simple to operate and very effective. The way it flashes in the sunlight is obvious from a great distance. You'd have to be asleep to miss it!)

One of the first things the men did after landing was to rig up an aerial so they could listen in to radio transmissions from Sydney. Some time later, the four men tried to get the radio transmitter working by driving the generator by hand. They rigged up one of the aircraft wheels as a driving pulley and joined their belts together as a makeshift driving belt. This system failed for two reasons: the belt kept breaking and they couldn't turn the wheel fast enough to generate the required power. As neither of these factors stopped them from trying, they ended up wasting a lot of energy. I guess at the time, it gave them something to focus on.

While stranded on the Glenelg River tidal flats, the Southern Cross *crew tried to get the radio-transmitter working by driving the generator by hand. They rigged up one of the aircraft wheels as a driving pulley and joined their belts together as a makeshift driving belt.*

There was a real irony in this situation because before (when they'd lost their aerial while flying) McWilliams could transmit but not receive. Now they could receive messages but not transmit, because they no longer had the advantage of a wind-driven generator to produce power. They were stuck on the ground and knew their position, but couldn't tell any one.

On their second night, McWilliams managed to pick up Sydney on short-wave. The men learned that a vessel was leaving Wyndham to search the Drysdale River, and that a plane would join the search from Derby. I'll bet their relief was mixed with a degree of frustration—they were stranded about half-way between those two points.

With signal fires burning and an ear out for radio messages, food was their next priority. But looking for tucker out there is not an easy task for a bunch of city blokes. Remember it was the wet season, which is both a good and a bad thing in this situation. Most importantly there's plenty of fresh water to drink. The down side of having lots of fresh water lying about is the insect life it attracts, particularly mosquitoes and sandflies.

When you're out looking for bush tucker you've basically got two choices: hunting or gathering. Or both, of course. Smithy and his men weren't exactly prepared for survival. All they had with them were matches, screwdrivers, a penknife and a couple of .32 automatic pistols. They did try to shoot some small doves, but that was a dismal failure, as Ulm described on Wednesday, 3 April, their third day on the mud flats:

*Dogs' balls (*Grewia retusifolia*) grow in abundance around the Glenelg River tidal flats where Smithy was forced to land the Southern Cross. The berries are very sweet and taste a bit like apple strudel with a hard seed in the centre.*

> *Litch and self now going stalking doves—wish us luck. No damned good—can't shoot worth a rap—anyhow a small dove is hard to hit with an automatic.*

Even if they had managed to hit the unfortunate bird, I can't imagine there being much left to cook after the .32 calibre bullet had done its job.

As they didn't have an axe, rifle or even a fishing line, and they had no way to trap food, all these blokes could do now was gather food. Between looking for food, keeping the signal fires going and trying to turn the generator, they were rapidly losing strength.

As Smithy wrote,

> *when people are shipwrecked on a desert island—in romances—they manage to find all sorts of nice things growing on trees; they catch beautiful fish, discover that almost every*

plant bears edible fruits, and generally feast like kings. Unfortunately for us, we had no such luck.

It's an interesting point that although luck can help, survival is all about knowledge and an inner strength: the will to survive. If you don't want to stay alive, you probably won't.

Mind you, their immediate surroundings weren't exactly enhancing the situation. Every time they went near the water, for instance, they'd sink to their waists in mud; and the estuaries were alive with saltwater crocodiles. Eventually they did find something to keep them going: *Nerita*, a kind of snail that climbs the trunks of the mangrove trees. Smithy described them as *very muddy to the taste, positively loathsome to eat.* It takes a fair few of them to make anything like a meal, and I suppose they could get boring. One day, for lunch and dinner, the four men ate 200 of these *Nerita*. Still, if that's all you've got to survive on, you have to overcome revulsion, boil them up and eat them. Mind you, 200 might be a bit much in one go.

Even these days a trip to the Kimberley coast should not be taken lightly; seasonal cyclones, huge tidal variations and a maze of offshore reefs and islands still provide challenges.

Actually there's a tastier animal that lives around that mangrove country. It's officially known as *Telescopium telescopium*, but I like to call it *Icecream conatus* because that's what it looks like. You find it sitting on top of the mud, just near the water channels in the mangrove swamps. It looks about the same size and shape as a small ice cream cone, which is why I've given it that name. You cook it on hot coals, break open the shell, and inside is green coloured flesh, curled around the contour of the shell. Chewing it is a bit like chewing calamari—well, that's what I tell myself.

On 4 April, their fourth day of 'Coffee Royal', Ulm recorded in his journal,

Heat unmerciful. We are really starving—keeping alive on 1½ cups gruel per day . . .

Mac is nearly out to it today but still joking.

All feeling gnawing hunger pains.

Smithy's super energy is wonderful, but even his unusual strength is failing.

Apart from the intense heat, lack of food and the over-abundance of flies and mosquitoes, something else plagued them, as Smithy described.

The absence of tobacco was a great trial. All four of us were smokers, and we tried all kinds of leaves and grasses in an attempt to produce some sort of smoke; but, of course, they were all horrible.

Back in the rest of Australia, when no further news was heard, plans for what would become Australia's largest aerial search were quickly laid. But where to start?

As luck would have it Mr H C Brinsmead, then Controller of Civil Aviation, had made a special study of the Kimberley area. He analysed MacWilliams's sequence of messages from the *Southern Cross* and correctly identified the first mission station as the Drysdale River Mission and the second as the Port George Mission. He immediately suggested that the search area should be in the vicinity of Port George.

But here's a twist to the story: before the four aviators had left Sydney, Ulm had signed a contract with Sun Newspapers Ltd, one of Sydney's largest newspaper companies at the time. The *Sun* would pay Smithy and Ulm £500 if their flight to England was faster than Bert Hinkler's 1928 England–Australia record of 15 days 2¼ hours, and £250 if it wasn't. Either way Ulm would supply the *Sun* with daily reports of their progress, problems and any other interesting developments. So Smithy and Ulm had a media contract to fulfil.

Apparently a couple of Sydney newspapers got their noses out of joint when they found out about Ulm's contract with the *Sun*. It wasn't long before stories were circulating that suggested that Smithy had stage-managed the forced landing as a publicity stunt to promote the fledgling airline company. As far as media warfare goes, this would have to be one of the lowest acts.

Meanwhile, when no further news had been heard from the missing aviators, a citizens' committee was formed and £4000 raised within a couple of hours. With these funds the *Canberra*, a well-known plane, was chartered along with pilot Les Holden to go and search for the *Southern Cross*. The chief of the *Sun* also chartered a search plane, which left Port Hedland for the Wyndham area next day. A few days later another aircraft was on the scene, and by the tenth day four planes were scouring the Port George area.

Aboriginal people from church missions to the south and north of the Glenelg River joined the search on foot. Tough going, I can tell you, especially during the wet. The missionary assistant, Mr Beard, and a couple of young Aboriginal men set out from Port George mission:

> There was a stream, swollen by the recent rains, and also several swamps to be crossed. Actually they had to walk ten miles upstream before they could even find a crossing, and as they were walking along, Beard slipped and struck his knee on a rock . . . Unfortunately, they were in a swamp and within seconds they were completely covered with mosquitoes. Albert says they were thicker than any he has even seen, and it was quickly decided that a sore leg was preferable to being eaten alive. It was certainly not Beard's day, for when they did find a place where they could cross the stream, he led the way and sank suddenly into waist-deep mud.

But worse was to come. A bloke called Keith Anderson who'd been a personal friend and colleague of Smithy's for many years decided to join in the search. Anderson, with his mate Bobby Hitchcock as navigator, left Sydney on 4 April to fly to Alice Springs, where they planned to refuel before continuing on to the Kimberley. Anderson was flying a Westland Widgeon 111, a two-seat parasol-wing monoplane which he'd called the *Kookaburra*. It was also made of wood, the fuselage covered with a thin ply skin and fabric, and the folding wing covered entirely in fabric. Anderson had fitted the seven metre plane, which was powered by an 80 horsepower Cirrus engine, with long-range fuel tanks for endurance flying. Seated in the open tandem cockpits, Anderson and Hitchcock set out from Alice Springs at dawn on 10 April on what was to be their last flight.

The weather was hot, with dust rising in a way that did not help flying much. Although the plane was overloaded by something like 180 kilograms, the men had only three litres of water and enough food for one day. They had no radio of any description, and no emergency rations. The only tools on board were for tinkering with the motor. The map they were using lacked detail of the land between central and north-western Australia, their compass was faulty and the plane's only engine was playing up. Navigation wouldn't have been a problem if they'd followed the Overland Telegraph Line from Alice Springs north to Newcastle Waters then turned west. Anderson was convinced that he knew roughly where Smithy and his men would be found; in the rush to join the aerial search for the national heroes he and Hitchcock took a shortcut across the Tanami Desert.

Imagine constructing an airstrip in this sort of environment with your bare hands.

I get the distinct feeling that Anderson was set to rescue his mate Smithy come what may; the fact that he would personally benefit in the nation's eyes from rescuing an Australian hero was a point that was probably not lost on him at the time.

Well, they were just south of Oodnadatta when the *Kookaburra* developed engine trouble and Anderson had to bring the plane down in a small clearing in the Tanami Desert, over near the old Wave Hill Station. It's isolated from everywhere.

Over the last 20 years I've crossed the Tanami by vehicle too many times to remember, and believe me, you should be well prepared. It's getting a lot more civilised these days, what with the goldmines that are operating around the area, and it's no longer the lonesome track that it once was. Even so, you should still not treat it lightly. At its western extremity the Tanami Desert merges into the Great Sandy and Gibson Deserts across the Western Australian border. The Stuart Highway roughly marks the eastern edge. Tanami landscape is peppered with spinifex, turpentine bushes and termite mounds, and there's precious little reliable water. It's a challenging environment, and if you somehow find yourself having to survive in it, you've got to know what you're about.

Back to our story. Apparently a push rod on one of the cylinders of the aircraft was loose and Hitchcock, the mechanic, needed to tighten it. This was not a new problem. It had occurred before, way back down the track—same push rod, same cylinder. So they had landed the tiny aircraft simply to take a spanner out and tighten up the noisy rod nut. It was probably no more than a five or ten minute job, and one that any backyard mechanic could have done.

Before they could take off again, the men had to clear a short runway. But the scrub in that area is mostly turpentine and acacia bush, which grow up tall, then dry out and break, leaving sharp stakes. Tough stuff—but it has to be to survive the desert climate. Trying to clear it by hand is a killer, literally, because you lose so much water with the effort you expend. So, if you don't drink enough to replace that loss, you dehydrate and get weaker and weaker. That's exactly what happened to Anderson and Hitchcock.

After a whole day spent clearing the trees and undergrowth, the men tried to take off, but the runway still wasn't long enough. They made several attempts to get airborne, and in the process punctured one of their tyres. The next day they ran out of water and became too weak to work. When they couldn't find water they resorted in sheer desperation to trying to drink their urine. The whole day-to-day tragedy was recorded in a rough diary that Anderson wrote on the fabric of the aircraft's tail:

10/4/29–/4/29

Force landed here 2.35 p.m. 10th April 1929. thru' push rod loosening No. 2 cylinder cutting out (as at Algebucking S.A. on 9/4/1929, but temporarily fixed K.V.A.) exhaust valve & 25% H.P. Cleared bit of runway here which turned out just insufficient or engine coincidentally lost power. Since 12/5/1929 all efforts, of course same next to nil, thru' having no water to drink except solutions of urine (with oil, petrol, methylate from compass) directed on obtaining sufficient power from engine to permit of successful take off. No take off able to be attempted since 11/4/29 due increased debility from thirst, heat, flies & dust. Left Stuart [Alice Springs] 7.15 a.m. local time and followed telegraph for 100 miles which was intention. Cut off then direct for point between Wave Hill & Ord River Downs. On a/c crosswinds & inaccurate compass & having practically only sun for guidance as large map showed a featureless desert determined to above or nor'ward of course which am sure have done. As was in air for 7 hours and am pretty confident had 'Duckpond' on my starboard, I figure my position to now be—

Finding water in the Tanami is difficult and in many places impossible. When you travel through desert country you should carry your own water supply and plenty of it. The 'Duckpond' that Anderson referred to is actually part of the Winnecke Creek system. It consists of a small number of water catchments that form part of the Winnecke Creek floodout country. Certainly enough to keep you alive; had he landed there he would have been all right as far as water is concerned. That's the way Duckponds used to be when I first started to travel through that country, but how

One of the water catchments towards the headwaters of the Winnecke Creek system.

time changes. Nowadays it's an Aboriginal outstation which is sometimes occupied, and has a track leading direct to Lajamanu or Hooker Creek. There's also a satellite community telephone system, so any pilot needing help around Duckponds these days would be well catered for.

But back to our story. Now we've got four men missing in the Kimberley and two in the Tanami Desert. We've also got the media machine churning up stories back in Sydney, speculating as to just how real Smithy's forced landing was. Finally, at about 10.00 am on 12 April, the crew of the *Canberra* spotted the *Southern Cross* from the air. As you can imagine, Smithy and his crew were ecstatic, especially when the *Canberra* dropped them some food. News of the discovery flashed round Australia. But at the same time there were increasing fears for Anderson and Hitchcock, and the *Canberra* (along with other search aircraft) was diverted to look for the *Kookaburra*.

At about 10.00 am, 12 April, the crew of the Canberra *spotted the* Southern Cross *from the air. As you can imagine, Smithy and his crew were ecstatic, especially when the* Canberra *dropped them some food.*

Back at the 'Coffee Royal' site, the men still had to wait for the mudflat to dry out and harden before they could attempt a take-off. During the next six days, a variety of small aircraft flew in food, medicine, fuel—even a journalist! Not only that, but Beard and his young Aboriginal companions arrived on foot from Port George Mission—

a distance of over 60 kilometres. They didn't know that Smithy and the crew had already been spotted by the *Canberra*.

On 21 April, Qantas pilot Lester Brain located the *Kookaburra* from an aircraft called the *Atalanta*. He and his crew could see a body lying under a wing of the plane. The other man was nowhere to be seen, but as they circled overhead the searchers dropped a drum of water in the hope that he was still alive. It was impossible to land another aircraft beside the *Kookaburra* in the small clearing, so a decision was made to send in a party by land. The team was led by Charles Eaton, who had accompanied Brain in the *Atalanta*. He took along three Aborigines from Wave Hill station, an old Buick, and twenty or so horses. He also had air support.

It was 26 April by the time the land party made it through to the *Kookaburra*. The man lying by the plane was Bobby Hitchcock. Daylight, one of the Aboriginal trackers, soon found Anderson's body about 400 metres to the south-west of the plane. Both Anderson and Hitchcock were buried where they lay.

Smithy and his men were devastated when they heard about the deaths of their mates. The media had whipped the public into a frenzy, and it was no surprise when the Australian Government set up a Royal Commission to hold an inquiry into what had become widely known as the 'Coffee Royal Affair'.

The inquiry dragged on for four weeks, but I'm glad to say that Smithy and Ulm were finally exonerated. Nevertheless, their reputations as Australian icons were badly tarnished. However, some really good things resulted from the whole disaster—at least with regard to air safety in Australia. From that time on, all pilots had to submit detailed flight plans before take-off. Certain regions of Australia were designated 'remote areas', and pilots were permitted to fly over them only when carrying specified survival items. Proper aeronautical charts were published so that pilots would have a better idea of where they were and the conditions they were likely to encounter.

Kingsford Smith, Ulm and the crew learned some hard lessons from their experience in the Kimberley. Next time they flew to England, the *Southern Cross* carried a few extra items: an emergency transmitter that worked on the ground as well as in the air, a complete range of tools, a shotgun, flares, lots of food and plenty of water. They weren't going to get caught a second time.

The CAGE expedition party at
Pantas Well, MacDonnell
Ranges; left to right: Errol
Coote (pilot), George
Sutherland (geologist and
prospector), Fred Colson (a
local Alice Springs bushman),
Fred Blakeley (expedition leader)
and Phil Taylor (mechanic).
Lasseter is sitting in front of
Colson.

CHAPTER EIGHT

LASSETER'S GOLD

THE LASSETER LEGEND has got to be the ultimate Boys' Own adventure story and I can always remember being terribly impressed with it when I was young. I first encountered the story in Ion Idriess's book, *Lasseter's Last Ride*. First published back in 1931, it was a fabulous tale of gold *as thick as plums in a pudding* in the desert area of Central Australia, and of the man—Harold Bell Lasseter—who died searching for it. At the time I believed every word, not understanding that the book's author was a man who didn't let the facts get in the way of a good story.

As time passed, the mystery of 'Lasseter's lost reef', as the story became known, stayed with me. In the early 1970s, when I was a platoon commander with the Australian Army, I was always on the lookout for interesting things for the soldiers to do. One day we decided that we'd mount an exercise to find Lasseter's reef. While I didn't hold high hopes for success, I knew that the challenges presented by Central Australia's desert country would provide excellent training for the men, and that the lure of a 'lost gold reef' would add a bit of incentive. We called the exercise 'Bob Buck' in memory of the bloke who eventually found Lasseter's body out in the Petermann Ranges. I was aware that Lasseter had a son also called Bob, and started my research by writing to him to find out some bits of information. Meanwhile, the wheels of army bureaucracy were turning, with the result that exercise 'Bob Buck' died in its infancy. You see, I was stationed in Queensland at the time, and as Central Australia lies in the Northern Territory—outside Queensland—approval was not granted.

Since then I've spent a fair bit of time in Central Australia and I've heard all sorts of tales about Lasseter and his reef. When the chance came to make a film about this yarn, I jumped at it. Once again, we turned to Bob Lasseter for assistance. He kindly agreed to meet the film crew on location and show us a number of spots that were significant to the story. This was the first time I had met Bob and I warmed to him straight away. During the course of our discussions I learned all manner of interesting details about his father and the lost gold reef.

Bob Lasseter stands beside the Lasseter Highway named in memory of his father who died while searching for a gold reef in Central Australia. The Lasseter Highway connects the Stuart Highway with the tourist town of Yulara out near Ayers Rock.

None of it makes much sense out of context, so let's travel back in time to 1930, when Australia was in the grip of the Great Depression. It was the toughest time this country has ever seen—a giant drop in the economy. Food, work and money were in short supply, and morale was at an all-time low. By then the Australian Workers' Union, originally formed in the 1890s, had become a powerful political force, with the nerve centre in Sydney.

One day, when John Bailey was president of the AWU, Harold Bell Lasseter

*Bob Lasseter inspects the cave
where his father spent almost a
month awaiting a rescue party
that never arrived.*

When the CAGE expedition set out from Alice Springs, Blakeley kept close enough to the spectacular MacDonnell Ranges to find water. With landmarks like this, it's pretty easy to stay on course.

The remains of ancient mountain ranges like these rise abruptly from the surrounding plains in the heart of the Australian continent.

This diary, which Lasseter kept during his search for the gold reef, later inspired author Ion Idriess to write Lasseter's Last Ride, published in 1931. It was the ultimate boys' own adventure story and I can always remember being terribly impressed with it when I was young.

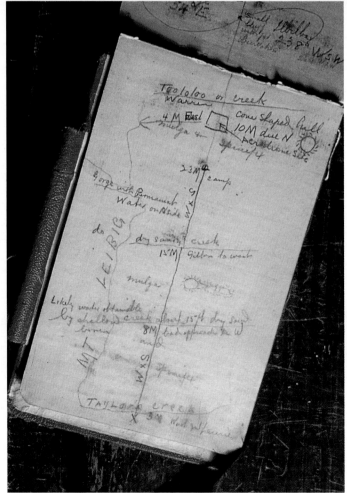

walked into his office looking for government assistance. He was out of work (that wasn't unusual, as most Australians had the same problem), but what he wanted was a bit different. He was hoping for funding to buy a few camels and enough food for a journey from Alice Springs way out to the West Australian border.

Now why on earth would anyone want to take on such a challenge, particularly in 1930 when most of that area was a blank on the map?

Lasseter's story really starts back at the turn of the century, when he was about 17 years old. He reckoned that in those days he was working on a ship off the Queensland coast when he heard about a recently discovered ruby field in Central Australia's MacDonnell Ranges. Thinking it was worth investigating, he left the ship in Cairns, bought some supplies and a couple of horses, and set off to try his luck. Many weeks later he reached the gemfield, only to find that the 'rubies' were actually ruby-coloured garnets—not worth a cracker. (The gemfield, near Alice Springs, is known as Ruby Gorge these days, and it's a local tourist attraction in the Centre.)

Apparently Lasseter thought he might as well continue on to the west coast. A map he'd seen showed that the MacDonnell Ranges stretched all the way there, and he figured he shouldn't have too much further to go. Weeks later he was still in desert country, with conditions getting worse by the day. When the MacDonnells petered out, a sea of red sandhills and spinifex confronted him. He pressed on, but his food supply was low and a few days later he ran out of water. Luckily for him, he soon reached more range country, and in the mulga scrub he found a waterhole.

While he was camped there, Lasseter noticed an arrangement of rocks that seemed a bit unusual. They were lying in a straight line and looked to him like spalls laid out for road making. In the old days, road bases were generally made by hand from rocks that the construction gangs had smashed up with sledgehammers. The smashed lumps of rock were called spalls. Anyway, Lasseter broke one of them open and to his astonishment found it contained gold. The line of rocks was part of a gold-bearing quartz reef that he reckoned he found broken up amongst the sandhills and mulga.

Lasseter collected a few samples and got going. A short while later, his horses died—starved to death. Now he was all alone with no idea how far he had to go. He ran out of water in the sandhill country and eventually passed out. When he came to, the first thing he saw was a very unfamiliar face. It belonged to an Afghan camel driver who helped him onto a camel and guided him to a camp belonging to a surveyor named Harding.

By this stage, all Lasseter had left was his bag of rock samples, and the clothes he was wearing. When Harding examined the samples, he was impressed enough to ask Lasseter to take him straight back to the quartz reef. But the whole ordeal had taken its toll on Lasseter and he had no desire to head back into that harsh country.

Instead, the men pressed on to Coolgardie. Lasseter and Harding went their separate ways, but stayed in touch. Harding was still keen to see the reef and a few years later again asked Lasseter to take him there. This time Lasseter agreed. They set out in an easterly direction from Carnarvon—about half-way up the west coast—with food, water and a few camels. It was a long, hard journey but finally Lasseter recognized some landmarks and found the reef. Its overall dimensions were impressive: about 16 kilometres long, ½ to 3½ metres wide, rising in places to a bit over a metre above the ground. The two men collected samples from different parts of the reef, took their bearings, and then returned to Carnarvon to stake a claim.

Back in Carnarvon their samples were assayed at about three ounces of gold to the ton—that was the good news. The bad news was that their watches had been out by an hour or so, which meant their bearings for the reef were incorrect. As the landmarks were so distinctive, Lasseter wasn't particularly worried.

You know, I've thought a lot about this part of the story because I find it quite puzzling. You see, if their watches were incorrect, then that would affect their longitude reading for sure, but it wouldn't make any difference to their latitude. So by rights, the reef should lie somewhere along their original latitude. Anyway, the story goes on.

For a while Lasseter and Harding tried to raise capital for a gold mining expedition, but there were no takers. In fact it was bad timing, because in the 1890s in Western Australia gold was there for the digging. The 1892 Coolgardie goldrush had lured people in droves, and the following year the Golden Mile—the world's richest reef—was discovered at Kalgoorlie. Compared with these and other successful gold mines, Lasseter's remote reef was peanuts—not worth the odds.

Well, Lasseter and Harding went their separate ways, and a few years later Harding died. Lasseter got on with his life. He worked on ships all around the world, spent time in England and Europe, and worked for some years in the USA. Back in Australia he moved around a bit, married, had children and turned his hand to all sorts of jobs, from cattle adjistment to house and boat building. He was clever and capable, with enormous amounts of energy, but at heart he was an ideas man whose ultimate vision was to create a better Australia.

By 1930, more than 30 years had passed since Lasseter had first seen the reef, out near the Western Australia–Northern Territory border. But he claimed to have been there twice, and said that the landmarks were deeply etched in his memory. He was convinced he could find the reef again. The men in the AWU office could scarcely believe their ears. A reef of those proportions would be worth millions, and finding it would end the Great Depression on the spot. This was just what Australia needed!

Things began to happen quickly. Over the next few weeks Bailey and his men called in a bunch of experts, a whole range of 'ologists', who gave all sorts of opinions. The well-known Sydney University geologist, Professor Sir Edgeworth David, reckoned there was no doubt that the area contained gold, as the country that extends to the borders of Western, Central and South Australia has the same geological characteristics as the country found round Kalgoorlie. But pilot Charles Ulm had his reservations. On hearing that Lasseter's watch had been out by an hour he said, *as the earth makes a complete revolution in 24 hours, it means from a longitude point of view, you were one-twenty-fourth of the earth's circumference out of place, which would put the reef somewhere in the Indian Ocean.* Ulm felt that 30 years was a long time, and that the landmarks would have to be a bit hazy in Lasseter's mind.

Many more meetings were held, the story examined from every angle, Lasseter questioned and cross-examined. Aside from the problem of the reef's exact location, his story was pronounced sound. But Bailey was waiting for word from Fred Blakeley, a bushman and prospector who'd spent a bit of time out that way. When both Blakeley and George Sutherland (a notable prospector) gave the thumbs up, Bailey and his men leapt into action. They agreed to form a company and float shares. No need for stockbrokers or share salesmen; ten blokes would get ten mates—100 shareholders all up—to put in around £20 each for an expedition to the gold reef. Ninety per cent of the profits from the reef would go to the shareholders and the remaining ten per cent to Lasseter. They called themselves the Central Australian Gold Exploration company— CAGE for short. There were seven company directors, and John Bailey was Chairman. Lasseter, who was not a director, would be paid a retainer of five pounds a week, and be on call for his services and information.

One of the CAGE directors was Errol Coote, a keen young journalist. With his help, news of the gold reef spread like wildfire; the phones ran hot and sponsors donated generously: a flash six-wheel, two-and-a-half-ton truck from Thornycroft Motors, petrol and oil from the Atlantic Oil Company, free transport on NSW rail— everyone pitched in to help. Coote, an enthusiastic but novice pilot, pushed the idea of aerial reconnaissance for the expedition. A light aircraft backed up by the truck would equip the CAGE expedition with state-of-the-art transport technology, and revolutionise remote-area gold mining. It was a bit different from Lasseter's original request for some assistance to buy camels and food.

The CAGE directors met to select expedition personnel. These expeditions that are put together by committees are always interesting. Lasseter would guide the team but not lead, as John Bailey had already picked Fred Blakeley for that job. Blakeley may not have been the ideal leader, but his brother, Mr Arthur Blakeley, was Federal Minister for Home and Territories. In other words, Arthur was in charge of Central Australia, so Fred got the job of expedition leader.

Blakeley's 55 year old mate, George Sutherland, was signed on as geologist and prospector. Coote, Blakeley's assistant, would buy and fly the company aeroplane. (Well, we'll see about the 'fly' bit later in the story.) Twenty-one year old Phil Taylor was the aircraft and motor vehicle mechanic. The sixth expedition member was a certain Captain Blakiston-Houston, ('Two Dads' for short because of his double-barrelled name) who was out from England working as aide-de-camp to the governor-general. He fancied a trip to Central Australia, had friends in high places and was willing to pitch in and do his bit. They were a motley lot, to say the least.

Coote paid £605 for a Gypsy Moth aircraft, recommended by Charles Ulm as easy to handle and in excellent condition. It had black wings, a red fuselage and undercarriage and soon sported its name—*Golden Quest*—in gold lettering.

Three months' worth of provisions were shipped by rail to Alice Springs, a remote outpost of civilisation and meeting point for the expedition members. Coote and Taylor would fly out in the *Golden Quest* while Lasseter took care of the Thornycroft. In Alice Springs Blakeley hired another of his mates, local bushman Fred Colson. For fuel and £3 a day, CAGE got the services of Colson and his Chevrolet truck and car. After wiring news of the latest changes to Sydney, the seven men left Alice Springs on 21 July 1930, vehicles loaded to the hilt. They even had a pushbike.

With its flashy aircraft, two-way radio sets, tons of supplies, guns, ammunition, vehicles—and the bicycle—the expedition attracted a lot of attention in the small settlement of Alice Springs.

At one of the outlying stations, Blakeley picked up an Aboriginal guide. Mickey was 45 and partly blind with sandy blight, but he knew the country ahead and could find water and bush tucker.

Soon the expedition was breaking new ground. It was heavy going; the country was in the middle of a drought, and to cross all the dry creek beds the men had to place strips of matting on the sand for the tyres to grip. Every so often they had to cut down tree branches to use for making tracks; I can tell you from bitter experience that constructing a 'corduroy track' is time consuming and back-breaking work.

Errol Coote, a director of the Central Australian Gold Exploration (CAGE) company, was the expedition's enthusiastic, but novice, pilot—pictured here in his flying rig, on the left beside the Golden Quest.

As the vehicles alternated between struggling through soft sand and bashing through bush, their high-revving engines overheated and began to use lots of water. After four days they reached a place called Dashwood Creek, which, according to Blakeley, *was a great bit of country with a big water supply; the water-hole was over four hundred yards long. Below the top of the sand it would last a big mob of cattle for months.* They made a fuel dump there, washed themselves and their clothes, and tested the wireless sets—which of course didn't work. A day or so later, they set off through thick mulga for Haast Bluff, a distant landmark.

Now mulga is really hard wood, as it's one of our *Acacias*—perfect for a warm fire in the middle of winter, but not much chop if you have to clear it out of the ground. I say that from personal experience; I carry around a small piece of mulga from that country—it ran up my shin about 15 years ago and broke off. I can feel it under my skin, a little hard lump attached to my shin bone. Strangely enough, the human body doesn't try to expel mulga splinters, the way it would with some other foreign bodies. The piece of mulga just sits there quietly, year after year, perfectly attached to my shin bone. By now the bone has completely grown over it.

When the men finally made it to Haast Bluff, about 200 kilometres west of Alice Springs, Blakeley and Lasseter had a serious falling out. Blakeley wanted to pass north of the monolith and then continue west, but Lasseter insisted his reef lay to the south-west. Blakeley was boss, so they went his way. Lasseter reckoned he was now 70 miles off route, and he wrote in his journal, *I wonder how the Directors expect me to find the reef if the leader will not follow my directions?* When you think about it, he's got a pretty good point there.

Blakeley's plan was to head for Ilbilla, in the Ehrenberg Range. The previous year the Mackay Aerial Expedition had made a base camp there, and Blakeley knew it had permanent water and an airfield. In due course he planned to send Coote back for the *Golden Quest*, and then they could start the aerial reconnaissance work.

The country between Haast Bluff and Ilbilla is characterised by mulga, sandhills and spinifex. If you happen to be travelling cross-country, the way they were, then you can expect to have a whole run of staked tyres, which is exactly what happened. Now, changing a flat tyre and then repairing it in the paddock is okay if it happens once or perhaps twice a day, but when it happens ten or twenty times, things get a bit frustrating, and it slows everything right down. According to Coote, *Our speed was so slow that even the flies could keep pace with us, and they attacked in millions. Everyone was fed up, tempers were raw.*

They got to Ilbilla about 7 August, and set up a base camp. From that point on things deteriorated. Mistrust between Lasseter, Blakeley and other expedition members deepened, arguments intensified, vehicles broke down, and of course the flat tyres just went on and on. Then Coote crashed the plane while attempting to take off from a makeshift runway at YaiYai Creek, about 130 kilometres east of Ilbilla. *'The air was hot and so was my temperature. I felt something was going to happen'*. He was right—he hit a gum tree and lost the left wing of the plane. As they had no communication system operating, it took some time for the others to find out that the *Golden Quest* was a write-off and that Coote was in Alice Springs recuperating.

Taylor and Sutherland with the wreck of the Golden Quest. *Coote crashed the plane at Yai Yai Creek, about 130 kilometres east of Ilbilla, while attempting to take off from a makeshift runway.*

Eventually the ground party pushed on about 150 kilometres due west, out near the Western Australian border. The time had come for Lasseter to get his bearings, and on 20 August he and Blakeley climbed to the top of Mount Marjorie in the Kintore Range, with an aneroid barometer, a sextant and three watches. According to Blakeley, *It was a brilliantly clear day and visibility was unlimited.*

Lasseter calculated they were now about 250 kilometres too far north. This would put the gold reef in the Petermann Ranges, but Blakeley reckoned he'd been out to the Petermanns and in his opinion there was no mineral-bearing country there at all. His suspicions about Lasseter were growing by the minute; the heat was intense, the truck more finicky than ever and enthusiasm was going downhill fast. Blakeley had had more than enough and ordered the whole party back to Ilbilla.

In late August, Coote and Pat Hall (a new pilot) arrived in the *Golden Quest II*, a smaller plane with a fuel range of about 560 kilometres. Coote was still recovering from his injuries, so next day Hall and Lasseter took off for the first reconnaissance flight and were away from camp for about two hours. During that time Lasseter reckoned he saw the reef, right in the heart of mulga country with no place to land a plane. As Hall later recalled, *we must have been gone about an hour and ten minutes when he started to jump about in the front cockpit very excitedly. He pointed at something, but I did not know what he was trying to tell me. He almost hopped out of the plane. There was no doubt that he was genuinely excited. Then he waved me to return.*

Flat-topped hills or mesas, are a feature of the Central Australian landscape. One of Lasseter's landmarks was such a hill, described by Lasseter as looking a bit like a Quakers Hat.

Before they'd left Sydney, Lasseter had promised the CAGE directors that he'd reveal his landmarks and the whereabouts of the reef once they were out past Alice Springs. By then, of course, he didn't trust Blakeley or any of his mates. But when Coote tackled him, Lasseter spilled the beans. He sat down and drew three hills in the sand with a stick. He reckoned they looked like women's sun bonnets (whatever they're supposed to look like) and that there was a fourth one 50 to 65 kilometres away that was a big flat-topped turn-out, a bit like a Quaker's hat. Strange descriptions; Lasseter must have had some sort of hang-up about funny-looking hats—can't understand it myself.

The *Golden Quest II* was now a little the worse for wear after bumping round on makeshift bush runways, so Coote and Hall flew to Adelaide for repairs. Finally, Blakeley agreed to push through to the south-west, the direction Lasseter had always wanted to go. But before long, the vehicle had completely broken down: sand in the engine, cylinders blown, crankshaft just hanging together. Ahead lay breakaway country and more sandhills, and already the truck was using lots of water. Under these circumstances, Blakeley again ordered the team back to Ilbilla. This time they only just made it, and as far as Blakeley was concerned, that was it—the expedition was finished.

But having got this far, Lasseter was absolutely determined to find his reef. As luck would have it a young German bloke called Paul Johns, who'd been scalping dingoes round the Musgrave and Petermann Ranges, materialised, *like a ghost out of the desert haze* with some camels. Johns had visited their Ilbilla camp some time before, so he knew all about the expedition and its various problems. Blakeley was more than happy for Lasseter to sign up Johns to accompany him in his search for the reef while Blakeley and the other expedition members returned to Alice Springs. In about mid-September the group split up. Lasseter, Johns and five camels set off for Lake Amadeus and the Olgas.

Meanwhile Coote was held up coming back from Adelaide, first by the repairs, then by strong headwinds that he struck in Oodnadatta:

For three days the gale blew, bringing huge clouds of dust that obliterated the landscape and filled the air with red dust to a height of 2000 feet.

He wired messages to Alice Springs and Sydney and was amazed to hear from Colson: *Expedition returning. Suggest you proceed directly to Sydney to avoid further expense.* This was followed by a message from CAGE letting him know that the expedition was returning without Lasseter, and asking him to proceed to Alice Springs, find Taylor, and then go out and make contact with Lasseter.

It took 13 days for Johns and Lasseter to reach Lake Amadeus. In that time, the two men lived on tinned salt beef, rice and just 70 litres of water, which is pretty

light going in desert country.

The first European to see Lake Amadeus was the explorer, Ernest Giles, in 1872. In fact it was this salt lake that prevented him from reaching the Olgas, which he could see in the distance:

the horses were all floundering about in the bottomless bed of this infernal lake . . . We were powerless to help them, for we could not get near owing to the bog, and we sank up over our knees, where the crust was broken, in hot salt mud.

The lake's glaring white salt surface is visible from at least 80 kilometres away, and Johns and Lasseter had just about had it when they got there. Instead of skirting the edge of the lake, they tried to take a short-cut across straight across the top—a terrible mistake that nearly cost them two camels. The hard, crusty surface looked safe enough, but looks can be deceptive. The middle of the lake was very boggy and the camels' loads were heavy. The two men had failed to understand and appreciate the salt lake environment.

By the time Johns and Lasseter reached the Olgas they'd all but died of thirst. They'd had no water for the last few days but now there was plenty, and according to Johns, *In a delirious ecstasy I*

Lasseter and Paul Johns loaded up a team of camels like these and set off from Ilbilla for Lake Amadeus and the Olgas in mid September 1930.

splashed water all over my face, drank it, rolled in it—laughed and shouted and cried then drank more.

As they travelled further west, doubts began to niggle at Johns, and he and Lasseter had a bit of a brawl. As far as Johns was concerned, *Lasseter . . . did not impress me as a man who knew the country, but rather as one who had read about it.* Now this appears to be a bit of a recurring theme when Lasseter gets into company with another person. First they set off to find the reef, then invariably there's a falling out, and finally Lasseter either chums up with someone else or he goes off alone.

Nevertheless they pressed on, but by the time they reached the Docker River area they were just about out of rations. It was time to head back to Ilbilla for fresh supplies. From there, Lasseter sent Johns to Alice Springs with letters to CAGE giving explicit details of how the company could follow him. He also arranged with Johns to return immediately with fresh camels and then follow him out, while he (Lasseter) set out alone with the two remaining camels. Johns was sure he could catch up with him in three weeks.

When you're moving through desert country, water is a number one survival priority. But if you've got camels with you, a little water soak is no good—you need to find decent sized rockholes. For that reason, Lasseter hugged the edge of the ranges as he headed west.

On 23 December he wrote in his diary,

I've pegged the reef and photographed the datum post on the Quartz Blow. The post is sticking in a waterhole and the photos face north.

Lasseter had always maintained that the only way to recognise the sun bonnets landmark was to approach them from the west, and he used a spot near Lake Christopher as a reference point. (We know he got that far because some years later a bloke called Michael Terry found a tree marked by Lasseter, and was told by the local Aborigines that a lone white man had once camped at the edge of Lake Christopher.)

The old blazed tree probably marked Lasseter's most westerly camp. Having finally found his reef again, now for the third time on the ground, as well as once from the air, he decided to head back to civilisation. At that stage his luck finally ran out, and in a big way: his two camels threw their loads and bolted. Stuck on a remote sand dune in Central Australia, all alone, he was desperate. He figured his best option was to hole up in a cave he knew about and await rescue.

As it happens, Lasseter had made a back-up plan to meet a mate of his, Olaf Johannsen, out at Lake Christopher. Lasseter knew that Johannsen, who'd be travelling from the west, would have no trouble recognising Lake Christopher because of its position right at the end of the range country, on the edge of the Gibson Desert. Lasseter had also sent the letter of instructions to CAGE with Paul Johns. The letter had asked for the follow-up party to travel to a gap in the Petermann Ranges and from there to follow the range country to Lake Christopher. And besides that, Lasseter was expecting Johns to return with the fresh camels from Alice Springs.

Up until this point, no one had ever heard of this bloke Johannsen—not the people on the expedition, nor the organisers back in Sydney, nor Paul Johns—no one except Lasseter. Yet suddenly we have this unknown person coming into the equation, and supposedly arriving from Western Australia. It's all very strange stuff.

Lasseter's cave was a godsend. You see, in the middle of summer, in the middle of Australia, shelter from the sun is imperative. The temperature inside the cave was about 15° cooler than the surroundings. With the help of some Aboriginal people he carried his remaining supplies from the sand dune to the cave and settled down to wait; someone was bound to come looking for him.

The cave was pretty well positioned, about 30 metres away from the dry bed of the Hull River. The Hull doesn't run very often, but in December 1930, Lasseter was able to obtain water by digging about half a metre below the surface. At the end of the hill in which the cave was formed, wild rock figs (*Ficus platypoda*) grew in abundance. And there were rabbits all over the place which he snared with fishing line or, occasionally, shot with his revolver.

It was unfortunate that Johns had taken Lasseter's rifle and left him with the revolver, because with a rifle Lasseter could have shot game more easily. The whole area had been in drought for several years, but the local Aboriginal people brought him food whenever they could. They encouraged him to eat and even tried to stop his dysentery. Lasseter reckoned there were something like 100 Aboriginal people in the area who came to look at the spectacle of the white man stranded in the cave.

I was really struck by the tragic side of the Lasseter legend when we went out to film the story for ABC TV.

At one stage he moved several kilometres upstream where rabbits were more plentiful, but there was no good shelter there, and the heat drove him back to the cave.

Health-wise it was a downward spiral for Lasseter. He found it hard to keep food down and was now in such poor condition he was almost beyond help. Apart from starving to death, he was nearly blind from sandy blight. After living in the cave for almost a month, Lasseter decided there was no way he was going to get rescued. The words he wrote are all contained in a diary—a series of letters he wrote to his wife—which he buried in the cave floor, just before he made one last dash for civilisation.

You can really gather the depth of Lasseter's desperation in these very personal thoughts that he wrote in the cave:

Dearest Rene I am sorry to finish out here and the worry of not knowing how you are faring and knowing how you must be in suspense as to my fate is simply the worst pain of all. Teach the children to believe the best you can of their father and soften the tale of my suffering here. If I could only know what the trouble is all about that no relief was sent or anything done at all. Oh it is awful indeed and the skeleton of me can hardly support the weight of my clothes. I'm an awful sight and the flies are maddening and ants something that Hell can not improve on.

So what had become of the back-up plans? Johannsen had (or was supposed to have) set out from Western Australia to meet Lasseter at Lake Christopher, but wasn't seen again. I guess we'll never be sure of what happened to him, but according to local rumour he was speared by Aborigines. As for Johns, apparently he didn't believe Lasseter would ever make it that far west and wasn't in any particular hurry to follow him up. As for Coote, he had managed to track down Taylor (the expedition's mechanic) in Alice Springs. They hired a few camels and a camel driver to take supplies out to Ayers Rock, which would be their new base camp. Taylor had agreed to fly out with Coote, but at the last minute, he decided to go with the camel team, as he was keen to photograph the landscape.

When Coote finally arrived at the Rock, there was no sign of Taylor or the camels. He flew back to Mount Connor, just in case they'd mistaken it for Ayers Rock, but they weren't there either. By the time he got back to the Rock he was almost out of fuel. Now, in Coote's defence, I've got to say that he was trying to land on a rough patch of open spinifex country right beside Ayers Rock, and there was no airstrip there in those days. He brought the aircraft down to earth, but guess what happened? This is how Coote describes the situation: *I had almost pulled up when a sound like a pistol shot made my blood run cold.* Jumping out of the plane, his worst fears were confirmed— he'd somehow managed to smash the propeller. *I was hundreds of miles from civilisation, entirely alone in the desert. My situation was precarious in the extreme.*

Meanwhile, Taylor was having his own dramas. Thunderstorms had turned the ground soft and boggy, and before long the small party was lost. It finally reached Coote on 7 November, about a month after leaving Alice Springs. Taylor repaired the damaged propeller, and Coote departed for Alice Springs and Adelaide saying, *Give me 12 days and, if I have not arrived back here, you make direct for Hermannsberg Mission.* In keeping with the run of bad luck, Taylor's camp and all his food burned down that same day.

Back in Sydney, hunger for gold was gnawing at the CAGE directors and shareholders. On 8 November, Coote arrived in Alice Springs and telegraphed the latest news to Sydney. No one was impressed and Coote was instructed to return to the Rock, pick up Taylor and fly back to Sydney. Coote, however, refused to go anywhere till a new propeller was sent to Alice. While he was waiting, Paul Johns showed up and recounted the story of his journey with Lasseter.

Coote wired this news to CAGE and was ordered back to Sydney. When he arrived in Sydney on 21 November the CAGE directors replaced him with a new pilot, Leslie Pittendrigh, and a mining engineer. The two men departed from Mascot airport in early December in the *Golden Quest II.*

Back to Taylor, he'd managed to get himself to Bob Buck's place, where he also contacted the directors. His instructions were to proceed to Ilbilla, reestablish a base there and await the arrival of the plane. He was then to go out and look for Lasseter. Taylor must have been a very patient sort of bloke—he seemed to spend a lot of his time waiting for people and planes that never showed up. By 26 December Taylor, still waiting, was really concerned. He got a message off to the Hermannsberg Mission, where there was a wireless set.

After a widespread aerial search the missing airmen were finally located at Dashwood Creek. Unable to find Ilbilla, they'd run out of fuel on their return flight to Alice

Springs—I told you these expeditions designed and run by committees were interesting!

During all of this to-ing and fro-ing, no one spared a thought for Harold Bell Lasseter. Eventually, in the middle of January, Johns and Taylor set out from Ilbilla to try to find him. Before long Taylor had developed a sore back and the two men returned to Hermannsberg, where Taylor commissioned Bob Buck to go and look for Lasseter.

Buck, who was a really experienced Central Australian bushman, followed Lasseter's tracks across to Lake Christopher via the Rawlinson Range. He then followed the trail back to the Petermanns, eventually finding Lasseter's body at a place that is today called Irving Creek. In April 1931 news of the find reached Sydney. Bailey penned a letter to Lasseter's wife, Rene, expressing the shareholders' sympathy and stating:

Each of the speakers stressed the fact that, notwithstanding so many doubters hitherto, all now admit that your husband's story with regard to the reef was absolutely true, and it is to be regretted that he was not spared to unearth the treasure which meant so much to Australia, and for which he gave his life.

Bob Lasseter had just turned six when news of his father's death made front page news around Australia. Since then, Bob and his family have had to live with the controversy, accusations and innuendos that followed.

Bob Lasseter accompanied us when we went out to film the story about the lost gold reef. Amongst the numerous locations he pinpointed for us with incredible accuracy, he showed us the exact spot where his father died. This spot is one of the prettiest I have seen in Central Australia. It's right beside a dry sandy creek with red rocky mountains in the distance, and in the fading afternoon light its beauty is hard to beat. Just have a think for a minute. Lasseter had staggered there over something like 50 kilometres in the middle of summer—January—been helped a lot by the local Aborigines, but finally given up. I guess if you're going to look around the landscape just before you die, you couldn't do much better. Forty-odd years later his son, Bob, found the precise spot and built a stone monument—again with Aboriginal help.

Harold Bell Lasseter was originally buried in 1931 at this remote site near Irving Creek. In 1957 a couple of American film makers dug up the body for reburial in the Alice Springs cemetery. I suppose the men meant well at the time, but I reckon they should have left things as they were.

Back in 1957 a couple of American film makers persuaded some Aboriginal people to show them the site of Lasseter's grave. Then, with no thought or feeling for the rest of the family, they dug up the body and had it reburied in the Alice Springs cemetery. I suppose the film makers meant well at the time, but I reckon they should have somehow left things as they were.

The trouble with gold is they say it gets into your blood—gold fever, they call it. I couldn't tell you how many people have headed out to find Lasseter's reef. And year after year they've come up with all sorts of theories as to where it might be. But the one man who knows more about it than anyone else alive is Bob Lasseter. He was just five years old when his father left home to search for the reef, but Bob still remembers

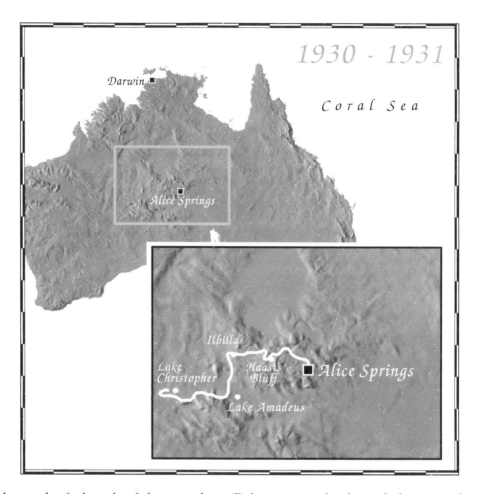

the words of advice his father gave him: 'Fight your own battles and always stand up for yourself'. He also remembers the map of Australia that his father put up on a wall in their family home when he was preparing to leave on his journey. While Bob's Dad was away, his mother would point out some of the places he'd be travelling to during the search for the reef.

When news of Lasseter's death reached Sydney and made national headlines, Bob had just turned six. Since then, he and his family have had to live with all the controversy, the accusations and (of course) the innuendos that followed. Determined to put the rumours to rest, Bob decided to mount his own campaign to find out the truth of the story. But he had no desire to be criticised for spending other people's money, so he worked hard and developed his own design engineering business, which was a great success.

In 1966 Bob finally made his first trip into Central Australia. Since then he's been back about a dozen times, mostly in a vehicle that was specially modified for long distance travelling in rough conditions. It's got a couple of boxes on the front for carrying spare oil, and tools for changing and repairing punctured tyres. To enable his vehicle to cross all the sand dunes in that part of the world, he fitted it with extra-wide tyres—Fokker Friendship aircraft tyres and rims—so the old Rover could just fly across the soft sand. But the most striking thing about the vehicle is the old bus seat on the roof. When you sit up there, you're about the same height Lasseter would have been on the back of a camel.

Bob got his pilot's licence in the 1970s and he reckons he's made dozens of reconnaissance flights and driven more than 10 000 kilometres off-road in his search for the gold reef. He's sure it's out there somewhere and that one day someone will find it. He really hopes that it happens in his lifetime and, better still, that he finds it himself.

I'll tell you something about Bob Lasseter: he can read a map. While he was on this trip of ours (filming the episode about his father) I asked him to point out on the map the location where he reckoned we'd find the old Ilbilla camp-site. He put a small dot on our 1:250 000 map of the area. According to Bob, we'd see the remains of the expedition there—things like old rusty drums and other bits and pieces from the CAGE expedition. Well, a week later I took off to find the location and set my GPS unit to the coordinates for Bob's dot on the map. After driving cross country for a few miles, I pulled up and the GPS said I should be right on the spot. When I opened the door of the Rover and got out, the first thing I saw was a pile of rusty old oil and petrol drums. There's no doubt about it—the man knows his map. I take my hat off to you, Bob Lasseter, and I wish you well.

Bob Lasseter's sure that the gold reef is out there somewhere and his skill and ingenuity may well see him find it.

BIBLIOGRAPHY AND FURTHER READING

AULD, W P., *Recollections of McDouall Stuart*, Sullivans Cove, Adelaide, 1984.

BEALE, EDGAR, *Kennedy Workbook: A critical analysis of the route of E.B. Kennedy's 1848 Exploration of Cape York Peninsula with a transcript of fragments of his journal*, Wollongong University College, 1970.

BEALE, EDGAR, *Kennedy of Cape York*, Rigby, Adelaide, 1970.

BEALE, EDGAR, *Kennedy The Barcoo and Beyond 1847: The Journals of Edmund Besley Court Kennedy and Alfred Allatson Turner with new information on Kennedy's Life*, Blubber Head Press, Hobart, 1983

BLAKELEY, FRED, *Lasseter's Dream Millions: New Light on the Lost Gold Reef*, Edited by FRANCES WHEELHOUSE and MARY MANSFIELD, Transpareon Press, Sydney, 1984.

BONYHADY, TIM, *Burke & Wills: From Melbourne to Myth*, David Ell Press Pty Ltd, Balmain, 1991

CAPELL, REV. ARTHUR, *Notes on the Warramunga of Central Australia*, Australian Institute of Aboriginal Studies, Sydney, 1963.

CARRON, WILLIAM, *Narrative of an expedition, undertaken under the direction of the late Mr Assistant Surveyor E.B. Kennedy, for the exploration of the country lying between Rockingham Bay and Cape York; by W Carron, one of the survivors of the expedition; to which are added, 1 The Statement of the aboriginal native Jackey Jackey, who accompanied Mr Kennedy; 2 The Statement of Dr Vallack and Captain Dobson who rescued the Survivors of the expedition; and 3 The Statement of Captain Simpson, of The Freak, who proceeded in search of Mr Kennedy's papers*, Kemp & Fairfax, Sydney, 1849.

COOTE, ERROL, *Hell's Airport: The Key to Lasseter's Gold Reef*, with Foreword by Air Commodore Sir Charles Kingsford Smith, Petermann Press, Sydney, 1934.

COMMONWEALTH OF AUSTRALIA, *Report of Air Inquiry Committee in Connexion with the Flights of Aeroplanes 'Southern Cross' and 'Kookaburra'*. March–April, 1929.

CRAWFORD, IAN MAXWELL, *The Art of the Wandjina; aboriginal cave paintings in Kimberley, W.A.* Published in Association with the WA Museum, Melbourne University Press, 1968.

DAVIS, PEDR and SMITH, DICK, *Kookaburra: the most compelling story in Australia's Aviation History*, Lansdown Press, Sydney, 1980.

FERGUSON, CHARLES D, *The Experiences of a forty-niner during thirty-four years' residence in California and Australia*. Edited by F.T. WALLACE, Williams Publishing Company, Cleveland, Ohio, 1888.

GROOM, ARTHUR, *I saw a Strange Land: Journeys in Central Australia*, Angus & Robertson, 1950.

HILL, ERNESTINE, *Paul John's Statement about Lasseter*, as told to E. Hill, Scrivener Press, Elizabeth SA, 1968.

KIMBER, R G, *Man from Arltunga: Walter Smith Australian Bushman*, Hesperian Press, Carlisle WA, 1986.

LASSETER, HAROLD BELL, *Diary, 1930*. (Unpublished version)

LEICHHARDT, DR LUDWIG, *Journal of an Overland Expedition in Australia, from Moreton Bay to Port Essington, a distance of upwards of 3000 miles, during the years 1844–1845*, T & W Boone, London, 1847.

MASLEN, T, *The Friend of Australia; or, A plan for exploring the Interior and for carrying on a survey of the whole continent of Australia. By a retired officer of the Hon. East India Company's Service*, Hurst, Chance & Co., London, 1830.

MCKENZIE, MAISIE, *The Road to Moanjum*, Angus and Robertson, Melbourne, 1969.

RODERICK, COLIN, *Leichhardt the Dauntless Explorer*, Angus & Robertson, North Ryde, NSW, 1988.

SMITH, SIR CHARLES KINGSFORD, *My Flying Life: An Authentic Biography prepared under the personal supervision of and from the diaries and papers of the late Sir Charles Kingsford Smith with a Preface by Geoffrey Rawson*, Andrew Melrose Ltd., London, 1937.

SPENCER, SIR WALTER BALDWIN and GILLEN, FRANCIS JAMES, *The Northern Tribes of Central Australia*, Ousterhout, The Netherlands, 1969.

SPILLETT, PETER GERALD, *Forsaken Settlement: an illustrated history of the settlement of Victoria, Port Essington, North Australia, 1838–1849*, Lansdowne Press, 1972.

SPROD, DAN, *Alexander Pearce of Macquarie Harbour: Convict—Bushranger—Cannibal*, Cat & Fiddle Press, Hobart, 1977.

STUART, JOHN MCDOUALL, *Explorations in Australia: The Journals of John McDouall Stuart during the years 1858, 1859, 1860, 1861 & 1862, when he fixed the centre of the continent and successfully crossed it from sea to sea*, Edited from Mr Stuart's manuscript by WILLIAM HARDMAN, Saunders, Otley & Co., London, 1864.

TIPPING, MARJORIE, *Ludwig Becker: artist and naturalist with the Burke and Wills Expedition*, Melbourne University Press, 1979.

TOLCHER, H M, *Drought or Deluge: Man in the Cooper's Creek Region*, Melbourne University Press, 1986.

WALSH, GRAHAME L, *Australia's Greatest Rock Art*, E.J. Brill—Robert Brown & Associates (Aust.) Pty. Ltd., In Association with QUEENSLAND NATIONAL PARKS AND WILDLIFE SERVICE, 1988

WEBSTER, MONA STUART, *John McDouall Stuart*, Melbourne University Press, 1958.

WILLS, WILLIAM, *A Successful Exploration through the Interior of Australia, from Melbourne to the Gulf of Carpentaria: From the Journals and Letters of William John Wills*, Richard Bentley, Publisher in Ordinary to Her Majesty, London, 1863.

The explorers in this book lived in imperial times, and they had to use the old imperial system of measurement—so here's a conversion table.

1 foot = 30.5 centimetres	1 hundredweight = 50.8 kilograms
1 mile = 1.61 kilometres	1 ton = 1.02 tonnes
1 ounce = 28.3 grams	1 gallon = 4.55 litres
1 pound = 454 grams	1 mile per hour = 1.61 kilometres per hour.

PICTURE CREDITS

INDEX